THE ATLAS OF EXPERIENCE

THE ATLAS OF EXPERIENCE

Louise van Swaaij and Jean Klare

English text version by David Winner

BLOOMSBURY

An atlas never just shows you where you are, where you want to go to and how to get there. It
also fires the imagination. Maps which chart rivers, mountains, towns, countries, far-away
regions, oceans and continents can arouse intense feelings. An atlas combines reality and
fantasy.

Maps evoke travel, exotic places and the allure of the unknown. Without a map, there would
be no way to know precisely where you are. There is no 'here' without 'there'. There is no
world without a map.

The Atlas of Experience maps a new yet familiar world. At first sight, the maps look like
ordinary representations of far-away places. On closer inspection, however, you will
realise that you are surveying our shared world of thoughts and emotions. This atlas is
based on traditional cartography, but it substitutes the names of cities, rivers and seas
for concepts, feelings and everyday experiences. Topographic concepts acquire symbolic
resonance.

Cradled by the Bay of Wisdom, the Sea of Plenty and Still Waters, lies a familiar and
barely traversible land with a capital, Growth, and airports, Escape and Freedom.
Everyone's experience is reflected in this world. You will find beautiful regions and
desolate ones: climb the MOUNTAINS OF WORK, survive the DESERT OF DESPAIR, visit
the ISLES OF FORGETFULNESS, be inspired by the STREAM OF IDEAS, pass through
border towns such as DOUBT AND FEAR. This strange island reflects that inex-
haustible adventure and journey called Life.

Our intentions are serious, but you can take the atlas lightly.

You can't really take a plane to the world of Experience, of course, because you already live
there. It's the place where you go through many changes on the way to Somewhere
Else.

Jean Klare and Louise van Swaaij conceived and laid out twenty-one countries in the
Experience. The maps show in detail the regions and cities of this world. Each depicts
a different theme and is accompanied by the philosophical reflections of David Winner.

The maps are drawn in Subjective Projection and reproduced in Unimaginable Scale.

Set out now on your own intriguing journey through this special atlas and experience an
original, refreshing and perhaps enlightening outlook on life.

CONTENTS

LEGEND

- Hamlet

- Village

○ Small town

● Large town

🏰 **CITY**

🏰 **CAPITAL**

IMPORTANT BUILDING,
OBJECT OF INTEREST

Darwin Lane   STREET NAME

LOVE   DISTRICT

BAY OF ^{SEA} WISDOM

🏭	POWER STATION	——•——•——	PIPELINE
🔊	NOISE	——•—•——	TERRITORY
🎵	SOUND	▪▪▪▪▪▪▪	BORDER
⚡	STORM	▪ ▪ ▪ ▪ ▪	LIGHT RAIL
♜	FORTRESS	▬ ▬ ▬ ▬	RAILROAD
✈	AIRPORT	———————	PATH
🗼	LIGHTHOUSE	——————	ROAD
🏭	FACTORY	═══════	HIGHWAY
🗼	WATCH-TOWER	∿∿	RIVER
▲	PEAK	∿⟍	RIVER WITH FLOOD BARRIER
🌋	VOLCANO	**H**	HIGH PRESSURE
🚢	SHIP OR FERRY	**L**	LOW PRESSURE
⚓	SUBMERGED WRECK	▲▲▲	FRONT
🚤	SUBMARINE	⬭	LAKE
⋰	RUINS	▨	BUILDINGS
∥	BRIDGE		

FARMLAND

HIGHLAND

MOUNTAINS

MOUNTAIN RANGE

BEACH

MARSHES

ICECAPS

DECIDUOUS FOREST

PINE-FOREST

SWAMPS

RAIN

CEMETERY

SHALLOW WATER

DEEP WATER

> 'And what are the dimensions of a revolution ...?'
> 'The dimensions, Your High Excellency?'
> 'Well, the length, breadth, and thickness, if you like it better.'
> Lewis Carroll, *Sylvie and Bruno*

Map-making is almost as old as human beings. 'The origin of the map is lost to history,' writes John Noble Wilford in his book *Mapmakers*. 'No one knows where or for what purpose someone got the first idea to draw a sketch to communicate a sense of place, some sense of *here* in relation to *there*. It must have been many millennia ago, probably before written language.'

Early Europeans drew maps on their cave walls, he tells us. Eskimos carved maps of their coast in ivory. In the Pacific, Marshall Islanders used sticks lashed together with fibres, coral and sea shells to represent prevailing winds, wave patterns and islands. On the maps of wheel-less pre-Columbian Aztec Mexico, roads were represented as lines of footprints.

In the last 100 years, the process of making maps has changed beyond recognition. Photographs from planes (and later spacecraft) changed the way we pictured the physical world and made ever-more detailed and complex maps possible. Now, computers can generate 3-D maps — and allow us to travel through them cybernetically. New places were mapped too: the moon, our neighbouring planets, distant galaxies. Simultaneously, map-makers have depicted cyberspace, deep oceans, the core of the earth, and mapped the tiny solar systems made of sub-atomic particles.

Medical science long ago charted the basic structures and systems of the body: the cardio-vascular system and our bones and muscles; the nervous and lymph systems. Soon the human genome will be visible. Scientists have even begun to map that most mysterious place of all, the inside of our brains. The so-called 'God Module' is the part of the brain which flares into activity whenever we think of matters spiritual.

Maps are usually considered as functional objects. They explain our surroundings to us and show us how to get to where we want to go. Yet they have always been highly evocative artefacts too, charged with poetry and fantasy. Marlow in Joseph Conrad's *Heart of Darkness*: 'When I was a little chap, I had a passion for maps. I would look for hours at South America, or Africa, or Australia, and lose myself in all the glories of exploration. At that time that there were many blank spaces on the earth, and when I saw one that looked particularly inviting on a map (but they all look like that) I would put my finger on it and say, "When I grow up I will go there".'

In the Middle Ages, lands beyond the borders of the map-makers'-knowledge were shown as full of dragons and exotic monsters. *Treasure Island* would have been a dull book without its map of hidden treasure. In one of his short stories, Borges conceived 'a map of the Empire that was of the same scale as the Empire'. There's a similar idea in Lewis

Carroll's *Sylvie and Bruno Concluded*: a map of the country made on a scale of a mile to a mile. The map, of course, could never be used. 'The farmers objected: they said it would cover the whole country and shut out the sunlight! So we now use the country itself, as its own map, and I assure you it does nearly as well.'

Even the most mundane-seeming maps can possess extraordinary poetic power and clues to a place's memories and soul. In *Rodinsky's Room*, Rachel Lichtenstein and Ian Sinclair tell the true story of David Rodinsky, a tragic and lonely Jewish man in the East End of London who vanished one day in the early 1960s. Nearly twenty years later, his one-room home above an old synagogue was rediscovered as he had left it, but crumbling into dust. Rodinsky had been dragged to a mental institution where he had soon died. One of the most potent objects he left behind was a copy of the London A-Z atlas which he had marked with ink. Sinclair later became obsessed with it. He described Rodinsky as a 'psychogeographer' and wrote a second book about his maps called *Dark Lanthorns*: '[Rodinsky] bent the maps to fit his notion of how London *should* be — if he was describing it for the first time. Maps were prompts rather than definitive statements. If a particular page took his fancy, Rodinsky would attack the margins with his red biro. Other districts ... were of no interest to him and they were ignored. He was a taxonomist, breaking down the overwhelming mass of information into categories that excited his attention: prisons, asylums, burial grounds of children's homes, hospitals. These markings become a projected autobiography, a Dickensian fable of abandonment, destitution and incarceration.'

One of the most famous of all American posters was Saul Steinberg's map of the world as seen by New Yorkers (Manhattan looming large and everything else in the world receding according to its cultural distance from the island). Even austere maps cry out for playful experimentation and reinterpretation. In *The Great Bear* the British artist Simon Patterson reworked the map of the London Underground and renamed lines and stations after philosophers, artists and soccer players. Upside-down world maps depicting Australia and New Zealand at the top of the world, and Europe and America at the bottom, adorn many office walls in the Southern hemisphere.

Meanwhile as old concepts crumble and new ideas are born in politics, the arts, religion and other areas of our lives, we look for new ways to describe ourselves to ourselves. It was perhaps only a matter of time before someone had the idea of playfully fusing classical cartography with the world of emotions, ideas and experience.

In 1999, the book called *Atlas van de Belevingswereld* (Atlas of the World of Experience) was a publishing sensation in Holland, becoming essential reading around the country and selling 100,000 copies in its first nine months.

English-speaking readers shouldn't think of this as a guide book. It's just a friendly companion for the latest stage of your most important journey: your journey through life.

SECRETS

MAP 1

'I hold this to be the highest task of a bond between two people: that each should stand guard over the solitude of the other. For, if it lies in the nature of indifference and of the crowd to recognise no solitude, then love and friendship are there for the purpose of continually providing the opportunity for solitude. And only those are the true sharings which rhythmically interrupt periods of deep isolation.'
Rainer Maria Rilke — *Letters to a Young Poet*

'I don't have anything personal. Nothing of value. No, nothing personal. Except my keys ...' That's the obsessively secretive Harry Caul speaking in *The Conversation*, cinema's most unnerving study of loneliness, voyeurism and technology. Harry is 'the best bugger on the West Coast', a technically brilliant surveillance expert who unthinkingly dabbles in the stuff of other people's souls, using his high-tech long-range microphones and electronic equipment.

Harry plunders other people's secrets; yet he keeps his own under lock and armed guard. When his landlady breaks into his home to leave him a birthday present, he feels violated and switches his mail to a post office box with a combination lock. When his mistress, Amy, says: 'I want to know you,' he reacts as if she were Hannibal Lecter and he Clarice Starling. Amy's questions are innocuous: 'Where do you live?' 'What do you do?' 'What's your phone number?' But Harry panics and scurries for cover: 'Why are you asking me all these questions? You never used to ask a lot of questions.' Locks can be picked, security systems breached. But the portals of Harry's heart are impregnable.

Harry Caul is a clinical case, but we all have our secrets. We need them. Our secrets are, in a sense, our truest, deepest selves, or at least, *keys* to our deepest selves. As children, we keep a secret diary and a secret hideaway to store our most private treasures. We have secret sweethearts and secret passwords. These secrets make us feel there is a part of ourselves that belongs to us alone. As teenagers, our bedroom is our inner sanctum and *no one* gets in without an invitation.

We live in a culture that has developed an insatiable appetite for secrets — as long as they are someone else's. In the universal *Truman Show* of the digital age, private intimacies are violated so brazenly and routinely we hardly notice it any more.

The American president and the British royal family were almost destroyed by illegally recorded telephone conversations. Paparazzi hunt the stars, and no biography is complete without revelations about its subject's sex life. This is the price of fame. Yet ordinary people have never been more willing to display themselves. Jerry Springer rules the airwaves and 40,000 people in Britain volunteered to be filmed twenty-four hours a day in the TV show *Big Brother*, a title which mocks George Orwell's nightmare vision of a world without privacy.

Harry Caul has a conscience. When he tapes an innocent-seeming conversation between two lovers, he worries about the moral consequences of his work and falters — only to be broken by an Even Bigger Brother. Meanwhile, one of the last American books published in the twentieth century was *I Listen*, a collection of private phone calls in which people unwittingly reveal their tormented relationships and sexual secrets for the amusement of the reading public. The calls were recorded illegally by a secretive 'techno music artist' known only as 'Spacewurm' who told a newspaper: 'You have no idea how addicting it is until you do it. Imagine being able to listen in on your neighbors, your friends and best of all, complete strangers in other cities. It's so easy, that's the best part. If you're smart enough to operate an AM radio you're half the way there. The other half is actually the harder part: being able to justify what you're doing, being able to handle the things you're hearing. For me, it's easy.'

Paradoxically, though, the more of these 'secrets' we hear, the lonelier and less connected to each other we seem to become. This is because there is a world of difference between secrets stolen and given freely as an act of love.

> *I will give you all my keys,*
> *You shall be my châtelaine,*
> *You shall enter as you please,*
> *As you please shall go again.*
>
> *When I hear you jingling through*
> *All the chambers of my soul,*
> *How I sit and laugh at you*
> *In your vain housekeeping rôle.*
>
> *Jealous of the smallest cover,*
> *Angry at the simpler door:*
> *Well, you anxious, inquisitive lover,*
> *Are you pleased with what's in store?*
>
> *D.H. Lawrence*

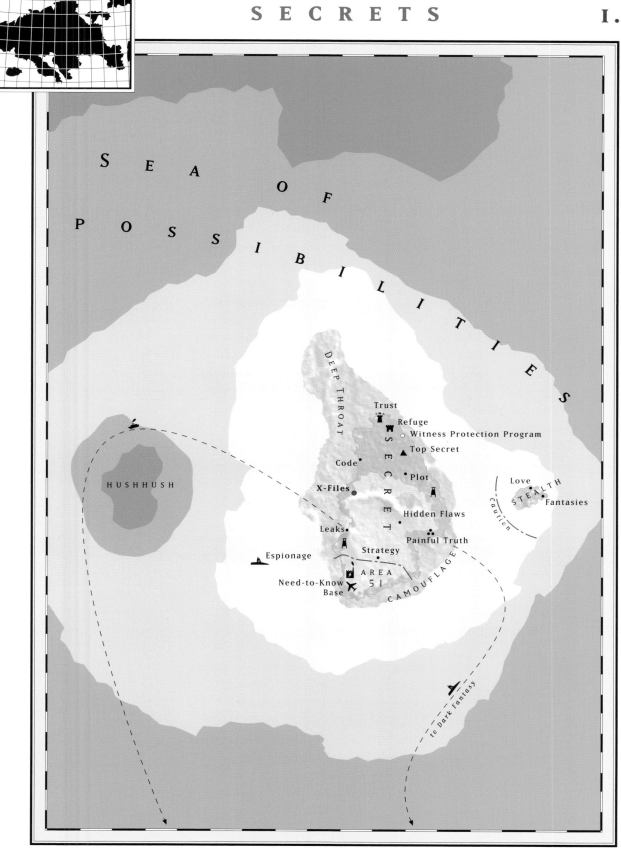

SEA OF POSSIBILITIES

DEEP THROAT

Trust

Refuge

○ Witness Protection Program

▲ Top Secret

S E C R E T

Code

Plot

X-Files

Hidden Flaws

Leaks

Painful Truth

Espionage

Strategy

Need-to-Know Base

A R E A 5 1

CAMOUFLAGE

Caution

Love

STEALTH

Fantasies

HUSHHUSH

to Dark Fantasy

p 17

SCALE

5   10   15   20   25

'In formulating any philosophy, the first question must always be: what can we know? That is, what can we be sure we know, or sure that we know we knew it, if it is indeed knowable. Or have we simply forgotten it and are too embarrassed to say anything?'
Woody Allen

'Well, whaddya know?' Sounds like a throwaway line from one of the heavies in *On The Waterfront*? Probably is. But, like they say in *Airplane*, that's not important right now. The point is that this small-looking question is actually very big. What *do* we know? How do we know it? How come that the more we know, the more we realise how little we understand? What else do we want to find out? Before you rush to buy a copy of Immanuel Kant's *Critique of Pure Reason*, here are a few pointers.

Common sense may be 'the collection of prejudices acquired by age eighteen' (Einstein). Yet we know what we know and, much of the time, that's good enough. According to common sense, the sun rises in the east and sets in the west, going on holiday is good for us, being ill is unhealthy, lightning does not strike twice in the same place and everything has a beginning, an end and a reason (except for God).

Most of our essential wisdom is picked up when are very young. In *All We Really Need To Know, We Learned In Kindergarten*, the American writer Robert Fulgham showed how deep the simplest advice from grown-ups can be: 'Share,' 'Say you're sorry when you hurt somebody,' 'Put things back where you found them,' 'When you go out into the world, watch out for traffic, hold hands, and stick together.'

Schools don't always advance the learning process. One day in 1994, the novelist Nick Hornby sat down and wrote on a single piece of paper everything he could remember having learned at his English grammar school between 1968 and 1975 in his eight least favourite subjects: mathematics, history, biology, chemistry, geography, physics, religious education, and economics and world affairs. This, after some 2,000 hours of tedious study, was what he remembered:

> Maths: Area of a circle is y r 2 . Circumference of a circle is 2 y r. y is 3.14 (approximately). R = radius. The radius is half the diameter. You have to look up sine, cos and tan in a log book.
>
> History: The Chartists had six points: universal suffrage, secret ballot and four others. Mr Huskisson was run over by a train.
>
> Biology: You dissect a frog by snipping up its stomach. Petri dish.
>
> Chemistry: Bunsen burner.
>
> Geography: The name of my geography teacher was 'Boggy' Lee.
>
> Physics: — .
>
> RE: — .

Economics and world affairs (A-level): The name of the American pilot shot down over the Soviet Union was Gary Powers. Cost push inflation. Demand pull inflation.

Albert Einstein (who knew a lot about knowing) said: 'Education is what remains after one has forgotten everything one learned in school.' So if we already know the good stuff (and we're not going to remember any of the facts we learn at school) what kind of knowledge should we be trying to discover?

In Bergman's *The Seventh Seal*, as Death and the Knight play their lethal game of chess on the stony beach, Death asks: 'What are you waiting for?' The Knight replies: 'Knowledge ... What will become of us, who want to believe but cannot? And what of those, who neither will nor can believe? I want knowledge. Not belief. Not surmise. But knowledge. I want God to put out His hand, show His face, speak to me.' Philosopher Bertrand Russell said three passions governed his life: 'The longing for love, the search for knowledge and unbearable pity for the suffering of mankind.'

But knowledge can be tricky stuff. Ever since Adam and Eve took the first tentative step towards a recipe for Mom's Apple Pie, humanity has been torn between a yearning for ever greater knowledge and an instinct for comforting ignorance, which is never far from cruelty. The Church persecuted Galileo for his heretical belief (the crazy man thought the earth moved around the sun, rather than the other way around), and the Inquisition burned people who were interested in the 'wrong' kind of knowledge. The Nazis started by burning thousands of books and ended by burning millions of people.

Is knowledge always a Good Thing? There are things we find out and then wish we didn't know. In the myth of Pandora's Box, human curiosity unleashes all the miseries and evils into the world.

Even Einstein, who wanted 'to know God's thoughts' and urged relentless enquiry ('the important thing is not to stop questioning. Curiosity has its own reason for existing') occasionally worried about the consequences. 'Two things are infinite: the universe and human stupidity; and I'm not sure about the universe,' he observed. And towards the end of his life, he bitterly regretted that his work towards uncovering the secrets of the universe had also paved the way for nuclear weapons: 'If only I had known, I should have become a watchmaker.'

Discovered
Unbelievable
Unknown
Presupposing
Covered-up
Experiment

Pushback frontiers

At-the-crossroad

C O I N C I D E N C E

Radical

Into-View

Evidence

Non-Fiction

Fusion
Cold

Revelati

D
E
E
P

S H A R P - W I T T E D

Verificati

Off the rails

Association

Sidetrack

Hypothesis

Illumination

To-the-bottom

Test

S E A   O F   F E R V O R

Analysis

Beaten Track

Method

Awareness

Dawning
C

High Standard

S C I E N

Speculate

C E

Self-confidence

P
U
Z
Z
L
E

I N T U I T I O N

Connection

Mystery

Side Issues

Order

U N D E R C U R R E N T

Self-organisatio

Hysteria

Contemplation

Disorder

Mirage
Madness

Icarus Airport

Raving

Proclaim

Delusions

Symbols

Stream of Idea

Clearsight

Vision

Revision

C L A R I T Y

Survey

Judgement

O F   W I S D O M

Conjecture

Yearning

Advice

Grasp

WISDOM

R A N G E   O F   E D U C A T I O N

to Secrets

Hallucination

Astray

Seclusion

Dark Fantasies

Eccentricity

Nonsense

Reverie

e; told you so

Einstein

B R A I N S T O R M

Disclose

W. Allen

Trackdown

Genius

Knowledge

Castles-in-the-Air

Foreknowledge

IGNORANCE

Run Wild

FANTASY

F O R E S T   O F

C U R I O S I T Y

Wish

-secret

Main Issues

Fabulous

Diligence

COMPOSITION

Invention

onstruct

C R E A T I V I T Y

FERMAT

Last Theorem

HMS Wiles

Shimura

Taniyama

Euler

Gauss

Sophie Germain

In the Middle Ages, we believed our lives were controlled by Providence. In recent centuries, as the idea of God began to falter, we have come to believe we are the masters (and mistresses) of our own destinies.

No longer pawns in some higher game, we decide how to live and how to behave. Our choices in life are limited only by our own imaginations: 'I want it all, I want it all, and I want it now,' as the Queen used to sing. (Well, Queen, anyway.)

Yet, somehow, we still go through our lives with a feeling of dissatisfaction. We seized the freedom to do what we wanted — and then found we didn't quite know what we wanted to do.

This is partly because life is not a simple struggle between pre-destiny and free will. There is another life-shaping force at work: the power of habit.

First we have habits. Later, habits have us. As the Talmud says: 'At first, habits are as light as a spider's web, but soon become as strong as cables.'

Habit rules our lives except for two key periods, when we behave badly. The times when we are swamped by our hormones and our neuroses are adolescence and the mid-life crisis. These are the times in our lives when we turn on our habits with the fervour and unreason of wild revolutionaries.

As an adolescent, Graham Greene suddenly became so fed up with his dull life that when he discovered his older brother's gun, he felt inspired to play a deadly game. He had read how bored White Russian officers put a bullet in their revolvers, spun the cylinder a couple of times, held the gun against their temples and squeezed the trigger. The chance of death was one in five. Greene liked the odds.

In his autobiography, *A Kind of Life*, he recalled: 'I pushed the barrel against my right ear and pulled the trigger. I heard a clicking sound and when I examined the cylinder, I discovered that the bullet could not have fired. It was in the next chamber. I remember feeling awkwardly happy, like when party lights are switched on in the dark and tiny street. My heart was pounding in my chest and life was offering me endless possibilities.' He repeated the experience: 'At quite long intervals I started to yearn for another dose of adrenalin ... Gradually this anaesthetic started to lose its effect and the whole experience left me with nothing but the brute stimulus of excitement ... I said goodbye for ever to the anaesthetic while spending the Christmas of 1923 at home in Berkhamsted. When I administered the fifth dose to myself, it occurred to me that I did not even feel excited any more; I pulled the trigger with such indifference it was like taking an aspirin.'

Even Russian roulette can become just a habit.

When we drift through life's habitual comings and goings long enough, the crisis of middle age becomes inevitable. We are too old to rebel against our parents, so we rebel against everything else we hold dear instead.

In puberty, we rebelled to become older. In middle age, we misbehave to be young again. Shakespeare understood: 'Age, I do abhor thee; Youth, I do adore thee.' Where we once found excitement and new identities through our music and clothes, now we try to spice up our lives with a new partner, job, car or even a new nose.

For the middle-aged neurotic, the equivalent of Greene's pubescent pistol is probably the bottle of poison which Faust kept close at hand during *his* mid-life crisis. Faust only had to hold the bottle with the firm intention of drinking it in order to feel better:

> *I look at you, and my grief is reduced.*
> *I reach for you, my urge is soothed.*
> *The tide of the spirit ebbs away little by little.*
> *I feel guided towards the open sea.*
> *The water shines by my side.*
> *A new day tempts me to a new beach.*

Goethe's Faust was a fictional character with a romantic solution to his problems. He made a pact with the Devil that would keep him young for twenty-four years. The condition was that he would not become attached to anything or anyone, or if he did, he would go to Hell. Instead of making a pact with the Devil, other men suffering from mid-life crisis find girlfriends who are twenty-four years younger. That keeps them young too. But Hell is never far away.

But whatever we do, habits will get us in the end, for every action contains the germ of a new habit.

The life of philosopher Immanuel Kant was governed by habits. For most of his adult life, the author of *The Critique of Pure Reason* allowed himself to be dragged along in a whirl of social distractions, friendships and love affairs. Well into his sixties, he changed things around completely. His final years were controlled by reason and regularity to such an extent that the citizens of Königsberg could set their watches by his daily constitutional.

We leave with the illusion that we enjoy free will. We don't. We have habits. The trick is to pick good ones.

> *Sow an act and you reap a habit*
> *Sow a habit and you reap a character*
> *Sow a character and you reap a destiny.*
> Proverb

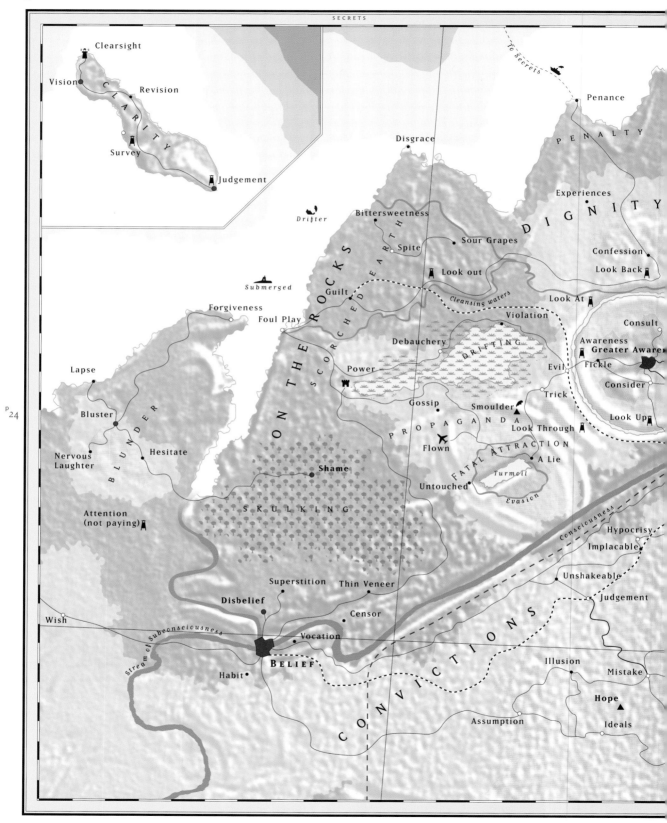

SECRETS

Clearsight

Vision

C L A R I T Y

Revision

Survey

Judgement

To Secrets

To Secrets

Penance

P E N A L T Y

Experiences

Disgrace

Drifter

Bittersweetness

Sour Grapes

D I G N I T Y

Confession

Spite

Look Back

Submerged

Guilt

S C O R C H E D   E A R T H

Look out

Cleansing waters

Look At

Violation

Consult

Forgiveness

Foul Play

Debauchery

D R I F T I N G

Awareness
Greater Aware

Power

Evil

Fickle

Lapse

O N   T H E   R O C K S

Gossip

Smoulder

Consider

Trick

Look Up

Bluster

B L U N D E R

Hesitate

P R O P A G A N D A

Flown

F A T A L   A T T R A C T I O N

Look Through

A Lie

Nervous
Laughter

Untouched

Turmoil

Evasion

Attention
(not paying)

Shame

S K U L K I N G

Consciousness

Hypocrisy

Implacable

Unshakeable

Superstition

Thin Veneer

Judgement

Disbelief

Wish

Stream of Subconsciousness

Censor

Vocation

C O N V I C T I O N S

Illusion

Mistake

B E L I E F

Habit

Hope

Assumption

Ideals

P24

SCALE

10   20   30   40   50

Belly-Flop

To Excuse

Brat

Naughty

Push

Splash

Y O U T H

Tree House

Cry

Mischief

See-Saw

Hide-
and Seek

Sly

Notion

Playtime

B A C K Y A R D

TO DINNER
IS READY

HOME

Discovered

Reservoir

Patience

nocence

Purity

Purification

Cancel

Conscience

Good

Target

Learn

'irtue

Unlearn

Look Across

Delay

Slacker

Duty

Look Down

Intention

Soon

D O I T

Challenge

Waving

Later
Opportunity

Own Way

Formed

Plans

Reputation

Overflowing

Top of the Pile

Submerge

Bragging

Bombast

Perhaps

Drowning

Immediately

Devise

Reckless

Distrust

Risk

Gamble

Up to you

Damage

Look Over

Luck

Daring

Neglect

Assure

Pride

COURAGE

R E A C T I O N

D O U B T S

C H O I C E S

Avoidance

Crossing the Line

Fame

Decision

Reflection

Guess

Discretion

Disillusion

Charm

Trust

N C E R T A I N T Y

Dependent

Tiny

Talent

H E A R T

Big Hearted

Emotion

PASSION

TO
ASSURANCE

TO
SELFCONFIDENCE

'The skeletons in the cupboard are coming home to roost.'
Tom Stoppard, *The Real Inspector Hound*

'Never play cards with a man named Doc. Never eat at a place called Mom's.'
Nelson Algren, *A Walk on the Wild Side*

Aunt Em had just come out of the house to water the cabbages when she looked up and saw Dorothy running toward her.
'My darling child!' she cried, folding the little girl in her arms and covering her face with kisses. 'Where in the world did you come from?'
'From the Land of Oz,' said Dorothy gravely. 'And here is Toto, too. And oh, Aunt Em! I'm so glad to be at home again!'
L. Frank Baum, *The Wizard of Oz*

'When I was home after my first tour, I'd wake up and there'd be nothing,' says the soul-ravaged, hallucinating Captain Willard at the beginning of *Apocalypse Now*. 'I hardly said a word to my wife until I said yes to a divorce. When I was here I wanted to be there. When I was there, all I could think of was getting back into the jungle.' The film which famously begins with 'The End' (the Doors song) is also haunted by homes and their destruction. When Willard watches his fellow Americans partying after destroying a village full of Vietnamese homes, he observes: 'The more they tried to make it just like home, the more they made everybody miss it ... The boys on the boat ... weren't looking for anything more than a way home. Trouble is, I'd been back there, and I knew that it just didn't exist any more.' When Mr Clean, youngest of the boys, is mortally wounded, the scene is made unbearable by the sound of his mother – the voice of his lost innocence and the home he will never see again – playing on a tape as he dies.

Home is a deep human need and a preoccupation. In childhood we need its security and love. In times of stress we ache to return. Psychoanalytic pioneer Erik H. Erikson, inventor of the concept of 'identity crisis', argued that children need a feeling of trust as they grow up. Yet even after an idyllic childhood, we all develop feelings of discord and nostalgia. Freud thought the paradise for which we long must be the womb. During the First World War, British tommies in the trenches sang with longing 'It's a long way to Tipperary / It's a long way to go. / It's a long way to Tipperary / To the sweetest girl I know. / Goodbye Piccadilly / Farewell Leicester Square ...' In *Jaws*, just before the giant shark attacks their tiny boat, Quint, Hooper and Brody sing: 'Show me the way to go home.'

Aching for home may be universal. But each person's home is unique and irreplaceable. 'I'm going to my home town – sorry but I can't take you,' sang Rory Gallagher. Some homes are mobile. Molluscs like Brian the snail in *The Magic Roundabout* carry their homes on their backs. The roving tribe rather than a physical location is home for a nomad. The Austrian-born American Henry Anatole Grunwald said home was 'the wallpaper above the bed, the family dinner table, the church bells in the morning, the bruised shins of the playground, the small fears that come with dusk, the streets and squares and monuments and shops that constitute one's first universe.'

Home may be where the heart is, but we have to leave one day in order to live and to grow. *The Jataka; or, Stories of the Buddha's Former Births* tells of a tragic tortoise who refused to leave his comfortable, watery home by the lake, even though he knew the lake would dry up one day. When a hot spell comes, he still refuses to move: 'I was born here, I have grown up here, and here is my parents' home. I cannot leave!' Instead, he digs a hole and hides, but is accidentally killed when the future Buddha comes digging for clay. Before he expires, the tortoise speaks:

> *Go where thou canst find happiness, where'er the place may be;*
> *Forest or village, there the wise both home and birthplace see;*
> *Go where there's life; nor stay at home for death to master thee.*

The ideal best thing is to leave home, follow your dreams and return enriched by the experience.

The Arabian Nights tells of a wealthy Baghdad merchant once blessed with a beautiful house and a fountain in his garden, who has fallen on hard times. Then he has a dream in which a mysterious figure tells him to go to Cairo where he will find a new fortune. He goes, but suffers only disappointment and hardship. Finally, when he tells a man in Cairo the reason for his journey, he is mocked: 'You idiot,' says the man, laughing. 'You foolishly travelled because of a dream which was nothing more than a meaningless hallucination. A man came in a dream too and told me about some house in Baghdad where a great sum of money is supposedly buried beneath a fountain in the garden. But I didn't go off on a wild goose chase. I stayed at home. Why don't you just go home?' So the man from Baghdad did. He went home immediately, dug up the fountain in his garden and discovered the treasure lying exactly where the man had described.

As Dorothy says at the end of *The Wizard of Oz*: 'If I ever decide again to seek my heart's desire, I won't look any further than my own backyard, because if it isn't there, then I never really lost it to begin with.'

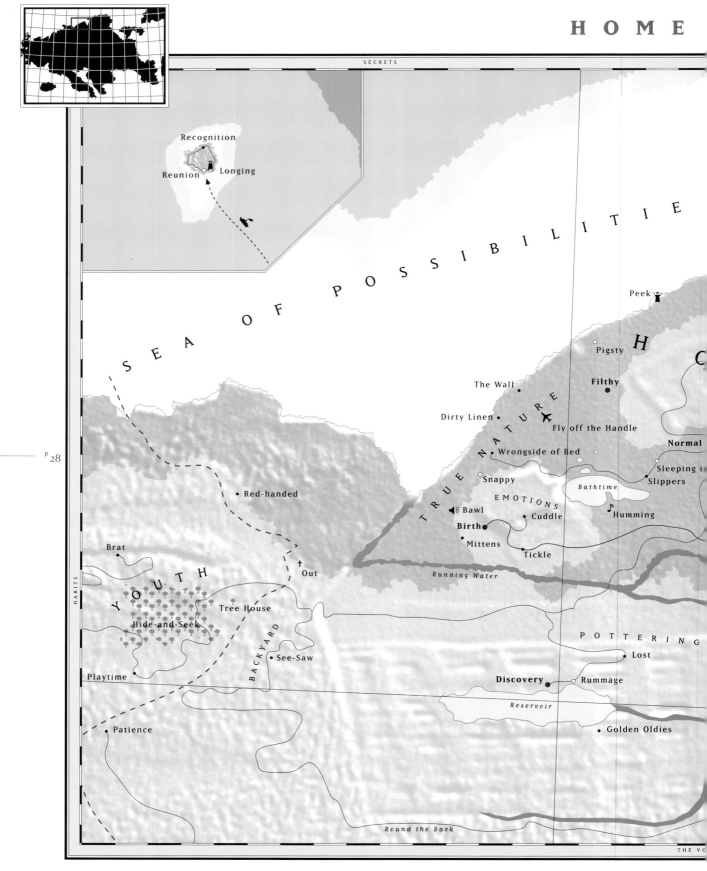

SECRETS

Recognition

Reunion • Longing

S E A   O F   P O S S I B I L I T I E

Peek

Pigsty

H

C

The Wall •

Filthy

Dirty Linen •

Fly off the Handle

Normal

Wrongside of Bed

Sleeping i
Slippers

Snappy

Bathtime

T R U E   N A T U R E

E M O T I O N S

Humming

◀ Bawl

• Cuddle

Birth

• Mittens

Tickle

• Red-handed

Running Water

Brat •

H A B I T S

Y O U T H

† Out

Tree House

Hide-and-Seek

B A C K Y A R D

P O T T E R I N G

• Lost

• See-Saw

Playtime

Discovery • Rummage

Reservoir

• Patience

• Golden Oldies

Round the Back

THE VO

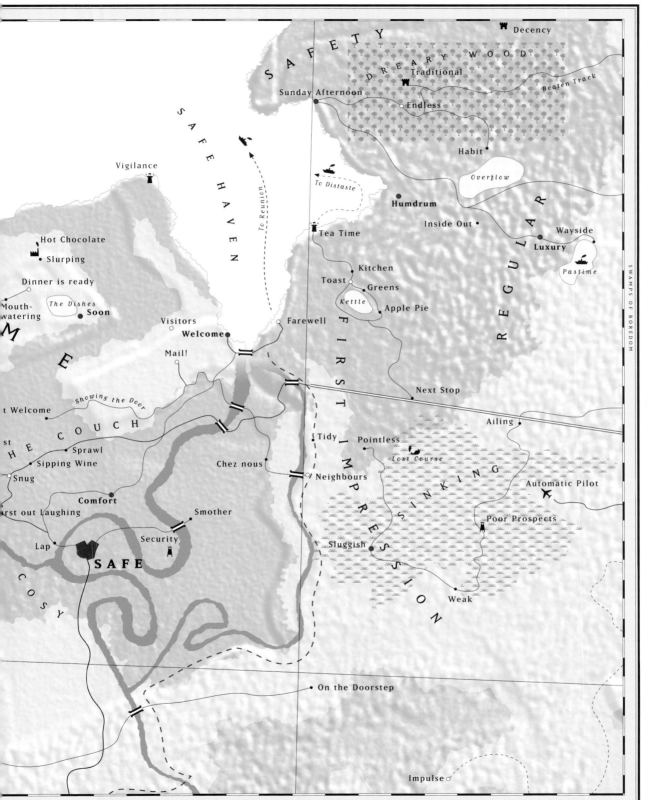

SAFETY

Decency

DREARY WOOD

Traditional

Beaten Track

Sunday Afternoon

Endless

Habit

Overflow

Vigilance

To Reunion

To Distaste

Humdrum

Inside Out

Wayside

REGULAR

Luxury

Tea Time

Pastime

Hot Chocolate

Slurping

Kitchen

Toast

Greens

Dinner is ready

Kettle

Apple Pie

Mouth-
watering

The Dishes

Soon

Visitors

Farewell

Welcome

Mail!

Next Stop

Showing the Door

Ailing

t Welcome

THE COUCH

Tidy

Pointless

st

Sprawl

Lost Course

Sipping Wine

Chez nous

Automatic Pilot

Snug

Neighbours

SINKING

rst out Laughing

Comfort

Poor Prospects

Smother

Lap

Security

Sluggish

SAFE

Weak

COSY

On the Doorstep

Impulse

SWAMPS OF BOREDOM

FIRST IMPRESSION

BOREDOM MAP 5

'Boredom is like a pitiless zooming in on the epidermis of time. Every instant is dilated and magnified like the pores of the face.'
Jean Baudrillard

'I spent a year in that town, one Sunday.'
Warwick Deeping

'The cure for boredom is curiosity. There is no cure for curiosity.'
Ellen Parr

Here are some boring statistics. Or, more accurately, some statistics *about* boredom, which is more interesting. The figures come from a study conducted by Cyber Dialogue, a New York-based research firm, and were reported in the January 1999 edition of *American Demographics* magazine:

21 per cent of Americans are regularly 'bored out of their mind'.

Most Americans respond to such boredom by switching TV channels.

44.4 per cent eat when they are bored.

27.3 per cent go for a drive.

8.9 per cent drink alcohol.

35.6 per cent feign illness.

19.4 per cent cancel subscriptions to boring magazines.

14 per cent take a vacation.

10.8 per cent have a haircut.

67.9 per cent say no time of the week is especially dull.

12.6 per cent say that Sundays are likely to be dull.

9.8 per cent say weekday afternoons are boring.

6.7 per cent are bored by week-nights.

1.9 per cent are bored by mornings.

33.7 per cent end boring relationships.

7.6 per cent cheat on their boring partners.

62.9 per cent of Americans are rarely bored.

16.2 per cent are never bored.

3.8 per cent seek counselling for boredom.

Bertrand Russell, the British philosopher, logician, essayist, social critic and author of books such as *Human Knowledge: Its Scope and Limits, The Conquest of Happiness* and *The Philosophy of Logical Atomism*, observed: 'Boredom is a vital problem for moralists since half the sins of mankind are caused by the fear of it.' Really half, Bertie? Precisely 50 per cent, you mean? Are you sure about that figure?

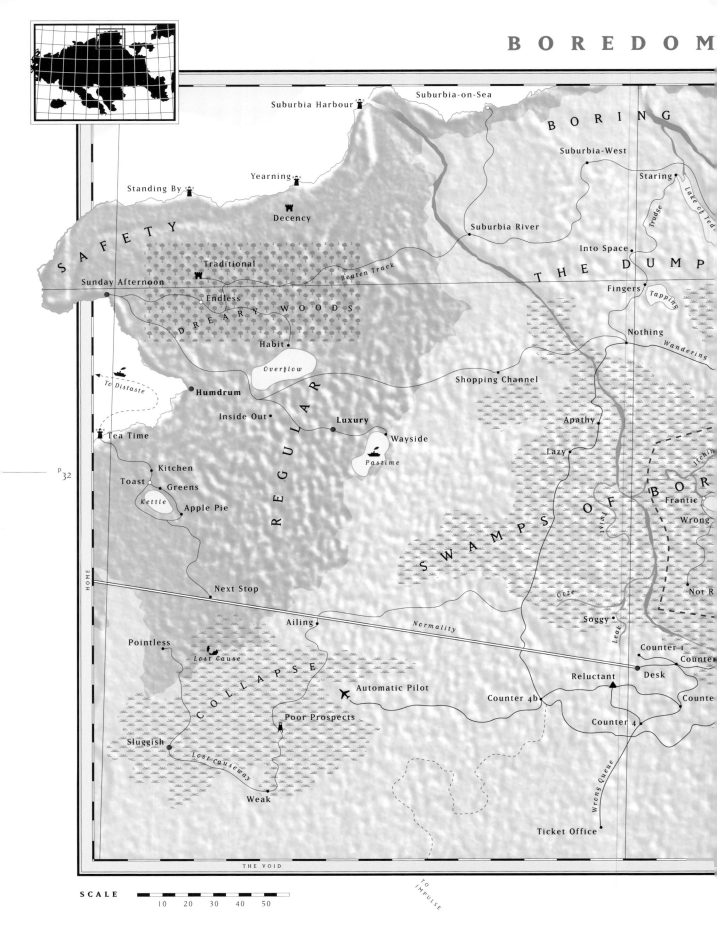

THE DUMP

BORING

Suburbia-on-Sea

Suburbia Harbour

Suburbia-West

Yearning

Staring

Standing By

Lake of Tea

Decency

Trudge

Suburbia River

Into Space

SAFETY

Traditional

Beaten Track

Fingers

Tapping

Sunday Afternoon

Endless

DREARY WOODS

Nothing

Wandering

Habit

Overflow

Shopping Channel

To Distaste

Humdrum

REGULAR

Apathy

Inside Out

Luxury

Lazy

Itching

Tea Time

Wayside

Frantic

Pastime

Kitchen

SWAMPS OF BOR

Wrong

Toast

Greens

Kettle

Apple Pie

Ooze

Soggy

Next Stop

Leak

Not-R

Ailing

Normality

Counter 1

Pointless

Counter

Lost Cause

Desk

COLLAPSE

Reluctant

Automatic Pilot

Counter 4b

Counter

Sluggish

Poor Prospects

Counter 4

Lost Causeway

Wrong Queue

Weak

Ticket Office

THE VOID

HOME

TO IMPULSE

SCALE

10 20 30 40 50

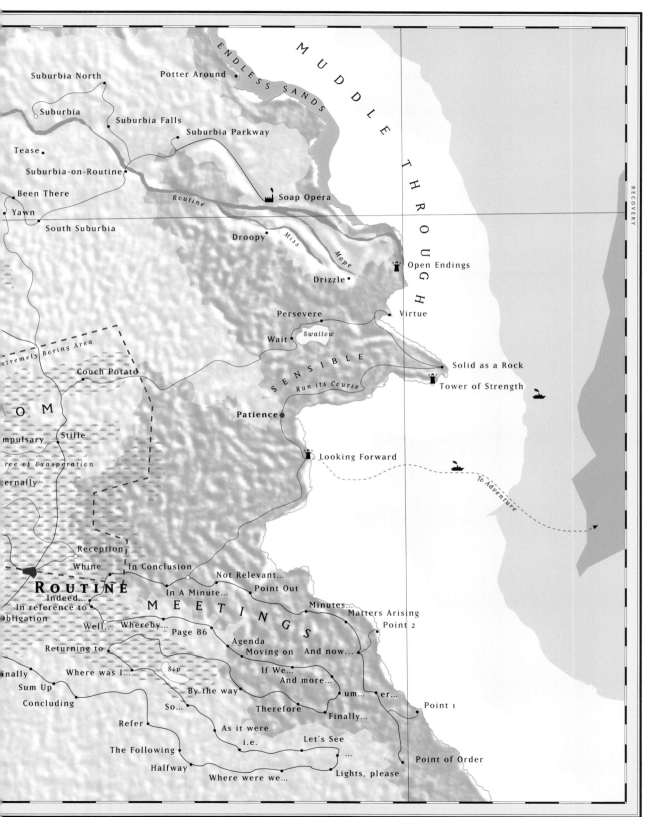

MUDDLE THROUGH

Suburbia North

Potter Around

ENDLESS SANDS

Suburbia

Suburbia Falls

Suburbia Parkway

Tease

Suburbia-on-Routine

Routine

Soap Opera

Been There

Yawn

South Suburbia

Droopy

Miss Mope

Open Endings

Drizzle

Persevere

Virtue

Wait

Swallow

SENSIBLE

Solid as a Rock

Extremely Boring Area

Run its Course

Tower of Strength

Couch Potato

O M

Patience

Looking Forward

To Adventure

mpulsary

Stifle

ree of Exasperation

ternally

Reception

Whine

In Conclusion

ROUTINE

Not Relevant...

Indeed...

Point Out

In reference to

In A Minute...

bligation

MEETINGS

Minutes...

Matters Arising

Well

Whereby...

Point 2

Returning to

Page 86

Agenda

inally

Where was I...

Sip

Moving on

And now...

Sum Up

If We...

And more...

Concluding

By the way

um...

er...

So...

Therefore

Point 1

Refer

As it were

Finally...

i.e.

The Following

Let's See

Halfway

...

Where were we...

Lights, please

Point of Order

'Illness is the night-side of life, a more onerous citizenship. Everyone who is born holds dual citizenship, in the kingdom of the well and the kingdom of the sick. Although we all prefer to use only the good passport, sooner or later each of us is obliged, at least for a spell, to identify ourselves as citizens of that other place.'
Susan Sontag, *Illness as Metaphor.*

Mary Lindsay (wife of the Mayor of New York): 'You look nice and cool, Yogi.'
Yogi Berra: 'Thanks. You don't look so hot yourself.'

The seventeenth-century British philosopher John Locke knew what was important in life: 'A sound mind in a sound body is a short but full description of a happy state in this World,' he declared. 'He that has these two, has little more to wish for; and he that wants either of them, will be little the better for anything else.' Or as Trudy Bernard (my grandmother) used to say much more succinctly: 'You should only be well.'

We all want to be healthy, as well as wealthy and wise. But it's easier said than done. After many centuries of medical research and countless generations of folk wisdom, we have begun to understand some of the basic ingredients of a healthy life. As long as you keep regular hours, eat a good and balanced diet, get plenty of exercise, think positive thoughts, avoid too much stress and have sex safely, you're in with a fair chance of being healthy. You should also try to get yourself some good genes and always stay clear of poisons, hostile micro-organisms, guns, wars, crime, fast cars, grizzly bears, earthquakes, exploding volcanoes and bad luck.

In *Sleeper*, Miles Monroe, owner of the Happy Carrot health food store in Greenwich Village, goes to hospital for a minor operation, wakes up 200 years later and finds it hard to believe that all his old friends have died: 'But they all ate organic rice!' In the twenty-second century Miles learns that things we think are bad for us (smoking, fatty foods, etc) are in fact ultra-healthy. The postmodernist cultural critic Richard Klein, debunker of health fads and author of the books *Cigarettes Are Sublime* and *Eat Fat*, has developed a similar thesis. As well as causing lung cancer, heart disease and many other horrible fatal illnesses, Klien insists: 'Smoking is praying ... The moment of taking a cigarette allows one to open a parenthesis in the time of ordinary experience, a space and time of heightened attention that give rise to a feeling of transcendence, evoked through the ritual of fire, smoke, cinder connecting hands lungs, breath, and mouth. It procures a little rush of infinity.' He has also argued: 'Life itself is a progressive disease from which we only recover posthumously; for if health is freedom from disease, then it is only available by dying. Living means choosing your poisons.' The tendency to ignore long term risks and live for the momentary pleasure of our vices can be irresistible. As Walter Bagehot said, 'The greatest pleasure in life is doing what people say you cannot do.' W.C. Fields knew the joys of keeping fit: 'Back in my rummy days, I used to shake for hours upon arising ... It was the only excercise I got.' The great film maker Luis Buñuel said: 'If the devil were to offer me a resurgence of what is commonly called vitality, I'd decline. "Just keep my liver and lungs in good working order," I'd reply, "so I can go on drinking and smoking."' And the Scottish folk singer Adam McNaughton is even more defiant in his song 'Cholesterol':

> Well, I don't give a hoot for her yoghurt and fruit
> I'll have Black Forest Gâteau and die.
> Cholesterol, cholesterol, my chance of surviving is small.
> The way that I dine, I'm on course for angina, but I love my
> cholesterol.

Even if you do want to do what's best, expert advice and the latest health research can be confusing. Around the turn of the millennium, the American media reported research studies showing that oestrogen therapy could lower the threat of heart disease and reduce the chances of developing Alzheimer's disease. A few months later new headlines warned that oestrogen therapy did not protect women from heart disease or slow the progress of Alzheimer's. And what about wine? Alcoholism and drunken driving may be bad. But, according to recent studies, wine-drinking may (or may not) reduce the risk of developing some types of cancer, kill some bacteria which cause food poisoning, lower susceptibility to osteoporosis and reduce the incidence of gallstones. Meanwhile, the jury's out on H_2O too. Water may be the stuff of life itself. But it has also been implicated in the vast majority of incidents of drowning.

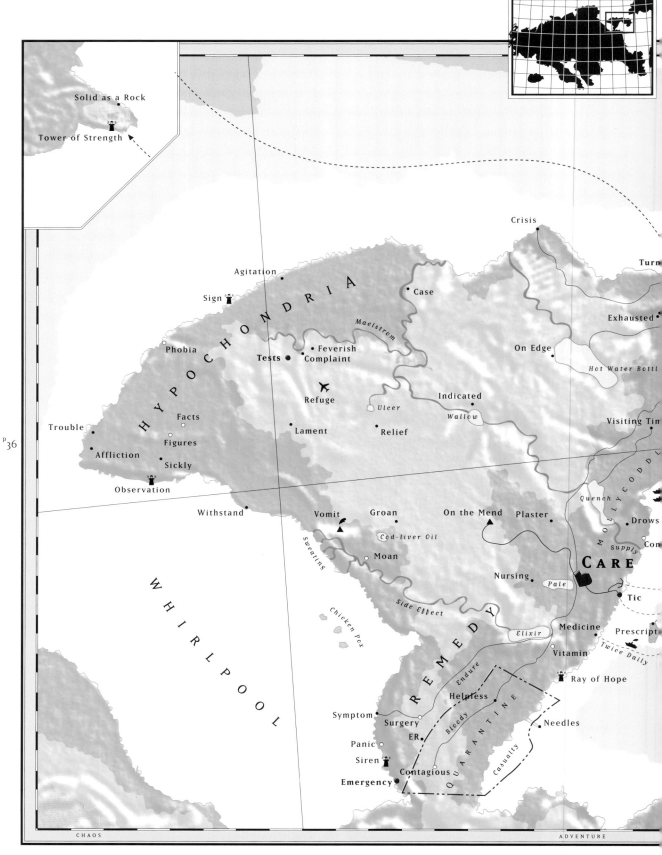

Solid as a Rock

Tower of Strength

Crisis

Turn

Agitation

Sign

Case

Exhausted

HYPOCHONDRIA

On Edge

Maelstrom

Phobia

Feverish
Complaint

Tests

Hot Water Bottl

Refuge

Indicated

Facts

Ulcer

Wallow

Visiting Tim

Trouble

Lament

Relief

Affliction

Figures

Sickly

Observation

MOLLYCODDL

Withstand

Vomit

Groan

On the Mend

Plaster

Drows

Cod-liver Oil

Supply

Con

Moan

CARE

Nursing

Pale

Sweats

Tic

Chicken Pox

Side Effect

Elixir

Medicine

Prescript

WHIRLPOOL

Twice Daily

Vitamin

REMEDY

Endure

Ray of Hope

Helpless

Symptom

Bloody

QUARANTINE

Needles

Surgery

Panic

ER

Siren

Casualty

Contagious

Emergency

CHAOS

ADVENTURE

SCALE

FROZEN WASTES

F R O Z E N
W A S T E S

S T O R M Y   C O A S T

Tremble

Bare-headed

Downpour

Windswept

S H I V E R

Whirlwind

Chattering Teeth

Sniffle

Fever

Ravaged

Delirious

Defy

Reserves

Warning Signs

Meanwhile

U N C O N S C I O U S

Clammy

Struggle

Gnashing Teeth

Knocked

Get Well Soon

Out

Anaesthetize

Suppress

tient

Going Under

py

Excuse

Smelling Salts

Revive

Sparkling

S H E L T E R

Ruddy

Fit

Glowing

Resistance

l Speed Ahead

You're frozen when your heart's not open
Madonna

The Queen in 'The Snow Queen', Hans Christian Andersen's haunting fable of aridity and the healing power of love, dwells in a vast, empty, cold place in the far north: 'The castle walls were built of driven snow, the windows and doors of piercing winds. There were more than a hundred rooms in the castle; the largest of them extending for miles and lit up by the lights of the Aurora. They were large and empty, icy cold and glittering.' At the heart of this bleak place is a frozen lake, 'cracked into a thousand pieces, each exactly like the others and each a work of art.' The Queen calls this lake the Mirror of Reason ...

In the story, Kay, a once-happy small boy, becomes hateful, callous and coldly clever when his eye and heart are pierced by two shards from a wicked hobgoblin's magic mirror. Later, Kay gets kidnapped (and kissed a lot) by the Snow Queen. She carries him off to her icy domain and holds him in erotic thrall. She teaches him 'reason', promises him the earth and sets him an infernal puzzle: if he can find a way to fit together the fragments of the frozen lake so that they spell out the word 'ETERNITY', the whole world (and a new pair of ice skates) will be his. This is, of course, impossible.

Luckily for Kay, his childhood sweetheart, Gerda, who is brave, loving and generous, arrives to rescue him. Gerda finds Kay in a dreadful state, blue with cold and still dragging around large, sharp pieces of ice in his bleak 'game of reason'. The story continues: '[Kay] sat quite still, stiff and cold. Then little Gerda wept hot tears, which fell on to his breast, and penetrated into his heart, and thawed the lump of ice and washed away the little piece of glass which had stuck there.' Kay bursts into tears of his own which wash the second piece of the evil mirror from his eye. He is cured! Finally, Kay and Gerda embrace, a sight which is 'so pleasing' that even the pieces of ice dance in celebration and, when they fall exhausted miraculously arrange themselves into the letters of the word 'ETERNITY'. Kay is truly free.

Intriguingly, the name Kay crops up again in *The Godfather*, that mighty twentieth-century epic of cold reason and frozen hearts. Here, Kay is a woman — the girlfriend (and later wife) of Michael Corleone, the film's tragic central figure. Francis Ford Coppola's story is darker than 'The Snow Queen', though, and his Kay proves powerless to save the man she loves during his journey from light to dark. At the beginning of the story, Michael is her engaging, warm and boyish lover. He ends the film as a loveless liar, and embodiment of cold, cruel power.

No magic mirrors are involved. Michael inflicts the damage on himself. We realise he's in trouble the moment he tells his brother: 'It's not personal, Sonny. It's strictly business.' His tragedy is that he thinks he must make himself cold and strong in order to protect the people and the family he loves. But his increasingly icy heart and chilly logic take him in the opposite direction. He is clever but not wise. The killing of Sollozzo, the assassination of the heads of the Five Families, and (later) the slaying of his own brother, Fredo, may all ultimately be good for business. But they have the effect of a car crash on Michael's soul. His mafia 'Family' goes from strength to strength. His emotional family is laid waste.

'Revenge is a dish best eaten cold,' as they say in Sicily. (They speak in similar terms of suet pudding in Macclesfield.) But Dante Alighieri, in his *Divine Comedy* about Heaven, Hell and Purgatory, warned that sins committed with a cold heart were worse — and are judged more harshly — than identical sins committed in the heat of passion.

Meanwhile, a cold persona — especially when coupled with a rigid devotion to harsh religious rules — is a recipe for unhappiness, as two other children, Fanny and Alexander Ekdahl, discover in Ingmar Bergman's movie *Fanny and Alexander*. When their father dies, the children's mother, a beautiful actress, remarries. It seems a fine match: her new husband is a respected local bishop. But life in his grey, castle-like home becomes hellish. The icy Bishop talks of obedience and duty and dispenses harsh 'discipline'. He is incapable of giving or receiving love. His domestic tyranny is in bitter contrast to the vibrant, chaotic, love-filled creativity and warmth of the large acting family they have left behind. The story is semi-autobiographical — Bergman's father was a pastor and Ingmar's childhood was desperately unhappy.

Yet, the bishop — like the Snow Queen and Michael Corleone — should be seen as a tragic figure rather than an evil one. 'Cold' people are usually sensitive souls who have suffered — or inadvertently inflicted suffering on themselves. As a result of hurt or loss, they take flight, withdrawing from the warmth of others to avoid being hurt again. Sigmund Freud and Melanie Klein identified this 'freezing' process as 'ego-splitting' and attributed to it lots of unhappiness-perpetuating personality disorders, such as narcissism, schizophrenia and the inability to form healthy long-term relationships.

As a psychic destination, the Frozen Wasteland has very little to recommend it. Fortunately, though, you can avoid ending up there by taking three relatively simple precautions:

1   Whenever you go to New York, do try, if at all possible, not to murder a leading member of any one of the Five Mafia Families.
2   Always stay away from mirrors made by hobgoblins (check label on back to make sure).
3   Never marry a bishop.

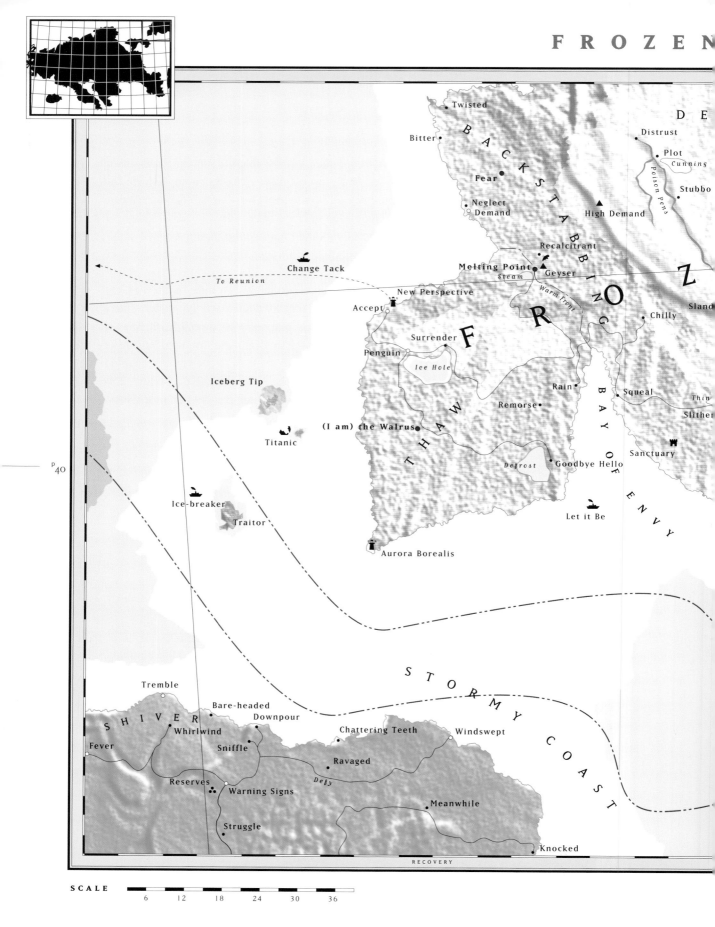

D E

Twisted

Bitter

B A C K S T A B B I N G

Distrust

Plot
Cunning

Poison Pens

Fear

Stubbo

Neglect
Demand

High Demand

Recalcitrant

Melting Point

Geyser

Steam

Change Tack

Warm Front

To Reunion

New Perspective

Z

O

Accept

Sland

Chilly

Surrender

F

Penguin

Ice Hole

R

Iceberg Tip

Rain

Squeal

Thin

(I am) the Walrus

Remorse

Slither

Titanic

T
H
A
W

B
A
Y

Sanctuary

Defrost

Goodbye Hello

Ice-breaker

Let it Be

O
F

Traitor

E
N
V
Y

p 40

Aurora Borealis

S
T
O
R
M
Y

Tremble

C
O
A
S
T

Bare-headed

S H I V E R

Downpour

Chattering Teeth

Windswept

Whirlwind

Fever

Sniffle

Ravaged

Reserves

Defy

Warning Signs

Meanwhile

Struggle

Knocked

SCALE

6   12   18   24   30   36

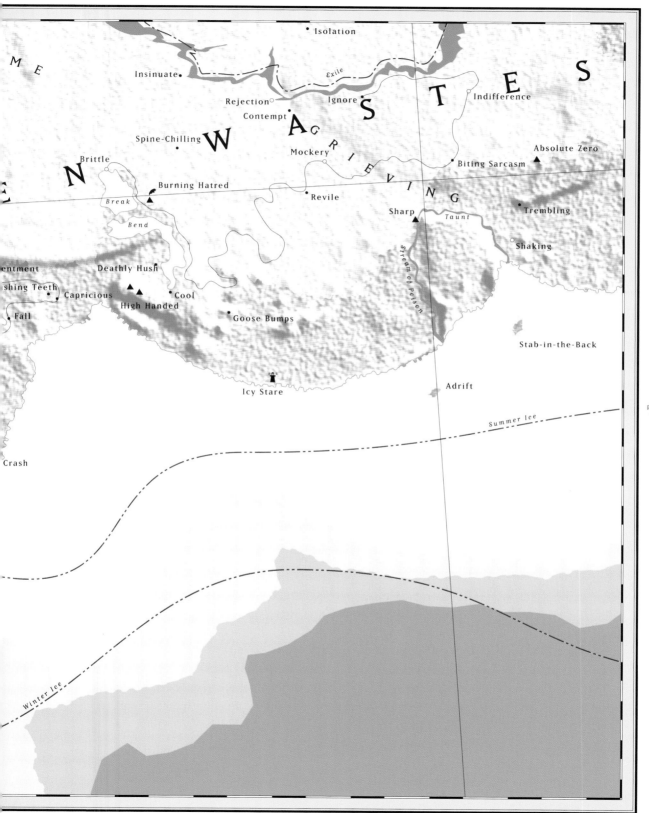

As any compiler of lists of uplifting quotations will tell you, 'Genius is one per cent inspiration and ninety-nine per cent perspiration.' On the other hand, you can sweat till
your washing machine breaks down and still be mediocre. You've got to have a Gift.

Think of all the hard-working musicians who perspire diligently for a lifetime without ever
coming up with something like the 'Hallelujah Chorus'. Then consider the case of the
man who wrote the 'Hallelujah Chorus'. George Frederick Handel's father was a bar-
ber-surgeon who hated music. He wanted his son to become a lawyer, and tried to suppress his talent, obliging George to practise secretly on a spinet harpsichord hidden in
the attic, each string wrapped with thin strips of cloth. As a young man, Handel moved
to England and wrote numerous operas and oratorios. He was successful and promi-
nent, but he was also mocked because of his fatness and heavily-accented English, and
he was often in financial trouble. By 1741, he was at one of his lowest points and was on
the verge of returning to Germany. Then a friend, Charles Jennens, asked him to com-
pose an oratorio based on a compilation of scriptures he had made. Handel agreed and
began work on 22 August.

Handel composed the *Messiah* in twenty-four days without once leaving his house. During
this time, his servant brought him food, and when he returned, found the meal was
often uneaten. While writing the 'Hallelujah Chorus', Handel was found with tears in
his eyes. He told his servant: 'I did think I did see all Heaven before me, and the great
God Himself!' Around the same time, Handel became devoutly religious, and started
going twice a day to church. Many years later, at a performance of the *Messiah* in hon-
our of his seventy-fourth birthday, Handel was feted and treated to thunderous
applause. He responded: 'Not from me, but from Heaven comes all.'

The *Messiah* may be one of the most sublime of all human works, but even at a less exalted
level, the process of artistic creation remains profoundly mysterious.

At the age of forty, the sixteenth-century French politician and author Michel de Montaigne
withdrew to his country estate, determined to worry about nothing except 'how to
spend the rest of my life in peace and seclusion'. He set his mind the task of becoming
'totally idle' so that it could 'find its own peace' He was hoping this wouldn't be difficult,
but he was wrong. 'The mind [which he called his "runaway horse"] gives itself many
more problems than it could ever bear for another. It causes me to experience so many
illusions and strange monsters, one after the other, without order and without sense. So
I started writing them down to consider them in all their oddity and absurdity, hoping
eventually to make it feel ashamed of itself.'

Unfortunately we don't have space here to explore the metaphysical conundrum of whether
Montaigne and Montaigne's mind (or horse) really were separate entities (though Steve

Martin's *The Man With Two Brains* explored similar terrain). Suffice to say that over the next twenty years, Montaigne entirely failed to tame his horse/mind/brain combo. Instead, he wisely allowed it/them to gallop away with itself/themselves, and, in the process, all of them together invented the Essay. Montaigne wrote more than a hundred celebrated and influential Essays with such diverse titles as 'Of Glory', 'Of Cannibals', 'Of the Resemblance of Children to Their Fathers' and 'That to Study Philosophy is to Learn to Die'. Montaigne also made a key discovery. He found that, when we focus on matters of the spirit rather than on a particular subject, we enter 'the indefinable world of imagination'. There we find more treasures than we could ever have suspected.

Samuel Taylor Coleridge provides the most famous case of doomed inspiration. In the summer of 1797, Coleridge, who had taken opium because he was suffering from dysentery, read this unpoetic account of the Mongol emperor: 'Kubla Kahn decreed the construction of a palace with an imposing garden. And so far ten miles of the fertile soil were surrounded by a wall.' Then Coleridge fell into a fitful, drugged sleep. For three hours as he drifted in and out of waking, two to three hundred lines of a new poem came to him effortlessly in pictures and phrases. When he got up, he could remember the entire poem. He gathered pen, ink, paper and started to write:

> *In Xanadu did Kubla Khan*
> *A stately pleasure-dome decree:*

Then he was interrupted by a visitor from Porlock who insisted on discussing a business matter. Coleridge had to talk for more than an hour, and when he returned to his writing, discovered that, apart from ten lines, the poem had disappeared from his mind 'like the images on the surface of a stream in which is cast a stone'. Fortunately, this new metaphor triggered a succession of images that enabled Coleridge to reconstruct parts of the vanished dream. This time, there was no visitor and Coleridge finished a new version of the poem.

The story has become a metaphor for thwarted brilliance. In Raymond F. Jones's science-fiction story 'Person from Porlock', aliens watch for signs of human creativity and, when they spot some, immediately send a person from Porlock to subvert them. In *Dirk Gently's Holistic Detective Agency* by Douglas Adams, a lover of the poem goes back in time and stands guard at Coleridge's door as he sleeps, determined to stop his visitor. He waits and waits and no one appears. Finally, worried, he knocks at the door to find out if anyone has somehow got past him ... and realises that he himself has become the Person from Porlock. The point is that genius or even genuine creativity (in whatever field) remains fragile and elusive. When it happens successfully, it ought to be celebrated. In song, perhaps, with an orchestra and a big choir ...

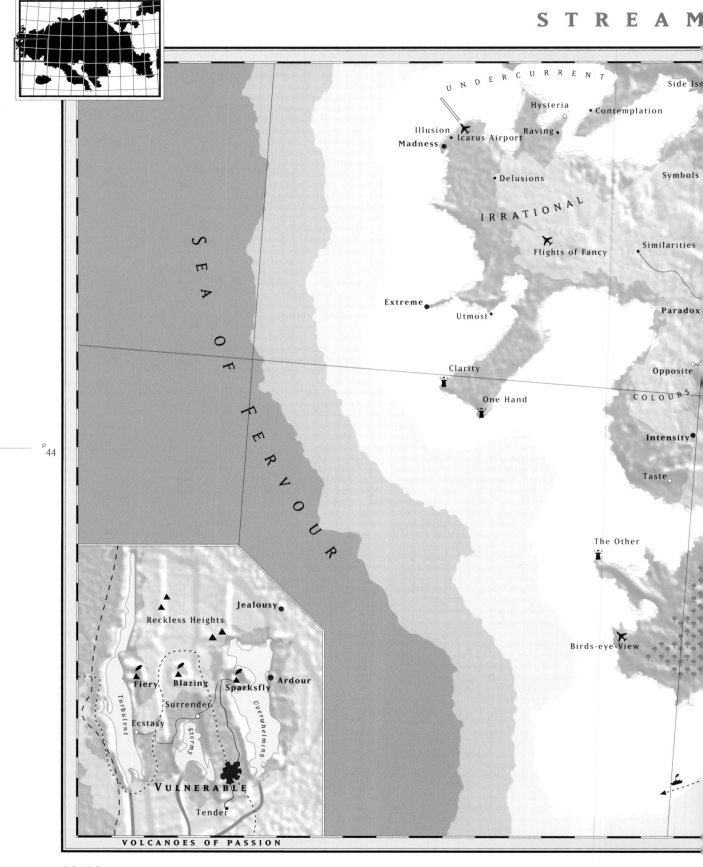

UNDERCURRENT

Side Iss

Hysteria

• Contemplation

Illusion   Raving

Madness   • Icarus Airport

• Delusions

I R R A T I O N A L

Symbols

Flights of Fancy

Similarities

Extreme

Utmost

Paradox

Clarity

Opposite

One Hand

C O L O U R S

Intensity

Taste

S E A   O F   F E R V O U R

The Other

Birds-eye-View

Jealousy

Reckless Heights

Ardour

Fiery   Blazing   Sparksfly

Surrender

Turbulent

Ecstasy

Stormy

Overwhelming

VULNERABLE

Tender

VOLCANOES OF PASSION

SCALE

0,1   0,2   0,3

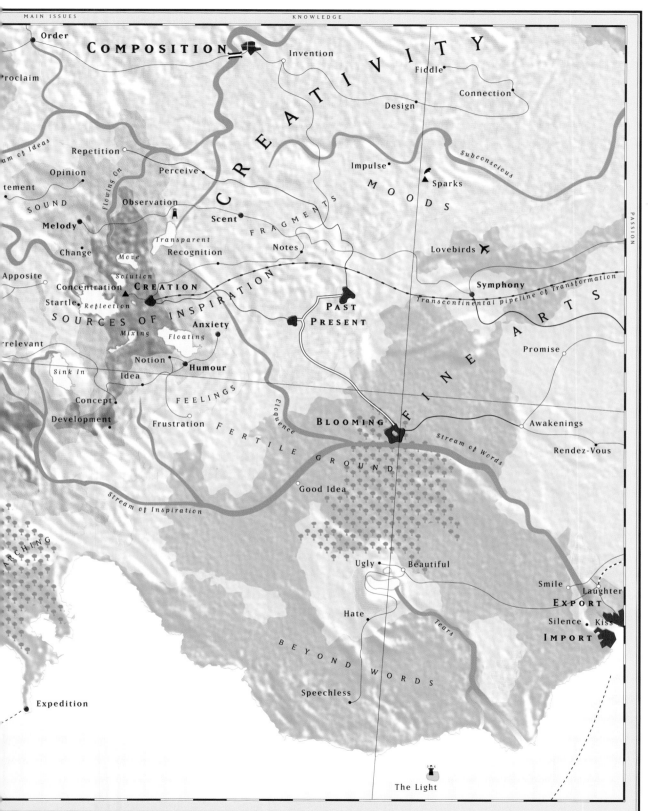

Order

COMPOSITION

Invention

Fiddle

CREATIVITY

Proclaim

Connection

Design

am of Ideas

Repetition

Subconscious

Opinion

Perceive

MOODS

tement

Flowing On

Impulse

SOUND

Observation

Sparks

Melody

Scent

FRAGMENTS

Change

Transparent

Recognition

Notes

Lovebirds

Move

Apposite

Solution

Symphony

Concentration

CREATION

Transcontinental pipeline of Transformation

Startle

Reflection

PAST

SOURCES OF INSPIRATION

PRESENT

FINE

Anxiety

Mixing

ARTS

rrelevant

Floating

Promise

Notion

Sink In

Humour

Idea

FEELINGS

Concept

Development

Frustration

FERTILE GROUND

BLOOMING

Awakenings

Stream of Words

Rendez-Vous

Eloquence

Stream of Inspiration

Good Idea

ARCHING

Ugly

Beautiful

Smile

Laughter

EXPORT

Hate

Silence

Kiss

IMPORT

Tears

BEYOND WORDS

Expedition

Speechless

The Light

PASSION

p
45

THE ISLES OF
FORGETFULNESS MAP 9

And I can't forget
I can't forget
I can't forget
But I don't remember what
Leonard Cohen.

According to a legend from the Talmud, children in the womb are wise beyond words. They are taught the Torah and then all the secrets of the universe are revealed to them. But at the moment of birth, an angel strikes them on the mouth and makes them forget everything. There's a similar idea in Plato's *Republic*: souls arrive in the world as falling stars and then, on the journey to life, must travel through a desert. By the time they reach Lethe, the River of Oblivion, they are thirsty, so they drink deeply from its memory-erasing waters. Some souls drink so much they immediately forget everything of their previous existence. Others, who drink more moderate quantities, retain a vague sense of their past lives. (These souls, said Plato, were the ones able to pass on something of their wisdom later in life. They become the world's philosophers, lovers and artists.) Or as Wordsworth put it:

Our birth is but a sleep and a forgetting:
The Soul that rises with us, our life's Star,
Hath had elsewhere its setting,
And cometh from afar:
Not in entire forgetfulness

To live is to forget. And it's better that way. If we remembered everything, our minds would be a nightmarish clutter. There have been cases recorded of people who forgot so little that their everyday lives were totally confused. There was no space for new thoughts or intelligent processing of information. Friedrich Nietzsche (how could we forget him?) believed that without forgetting there could be no happiness, no hope, no here and now. 'Whoever thinks much and to good purpose easily forgets his own experiences, but not the thoughts which these experiences have called forth.'

If people remembered everything, secretaries and diary manufacturers would be out of jobs. Moreover, the individual's tendency to forget has been one of the motors of human culture and creativity. Once upon a time, stories were passed down orally from generation to generation. Eventually there were too many stories to remember them all, so writing was invented to record them. Books came later. Then libraries, archives, data banks, and, eventually, the Internet.

If human beings were computers (which we aren't) we might compare our memories to hard-drives which slowly but surely fill up with old files and file fragments as we get older. And the older we become, the more difficult it gets for us to process new knowledge and experience. Older people remember events of thirty years ago more clearly than those of last week. The American writer and psychologist Lawrence LeShan observes that, for the first fifty years of our lives, we remember the details of the tasks we have to perform. But after the age of about sixty we see the world differently. We focus more on relationships and meanings. Our memory becomes more selective. Instead of remembering the names of the people we have just met, we focus on the emotional tone of the meeting. Instead of facts, we remember meaning. Instead of width, we remember depth. We lose the sharp edges of our memory; but that just makes us wiser and more able to put things into perspective.

Living is forgetting and forgetting is selecting. We come into the world as a blank page and leave it fully written. For most of us, absent-mindedness and oblivion are probably all we have to look forward to.

Don't remember where you put your keys? Don't worry. Think of it as your contribution to the advance of human civilisation.

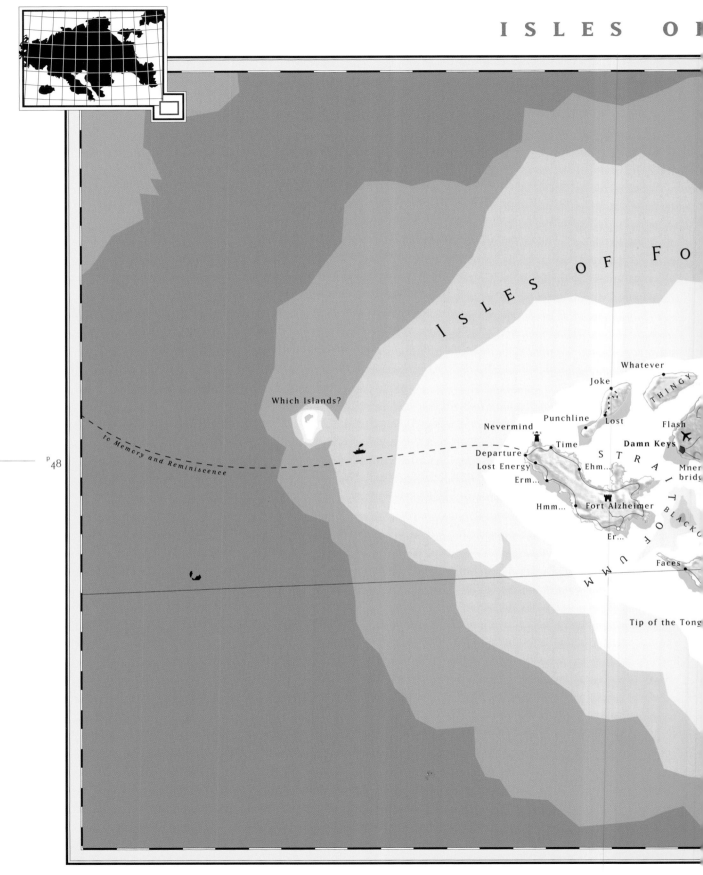

ISLES OF FO

Which Islands?

to Memory and Reminiscence

Whatever

Joke

THINGY

Punchline   Lost   Flash

Nevermind   Damn Keys

Time

Departure   S

Lost Energy   Ehm...   Mner...
                                      bridg
Erm...

Hmm...   Fort Alzheimer   BLACKU

Er...

Faces

Tip of the Tong

ETFULNESS

niversary

Pincode

Test   Mother's Day

THEMATICS
          Yourname
AMES   Firstname
          Surname
Whatshisname

TRAITS OF

intment

STRAITS OF . . .

'To be able to say how much one loves, is to love but a little,' said Petrarch, spot on on the question of the incompatibility of scorching passion and taking a rational approach.

That's the whole point of passion: to be the total opposite of cool reason.

Passion drags us to the Realm of the Senses, a land to which Logic can't even get a tourist visa.

'You shake my nerves and rattle my brain / Too much love drives a man insane,' noted Jerry Lee Lewis, from the male perspective, in his seminal work, 'Great Balls of Fire'. A similar sense of delicious, exultant, scrambled senses emerges from the poems of Sappho: 'As soon as I see you, even for a moment, I can no longer utter a single word. My voice falters. I feel a sudden burning under my skin as if touched by raging fire. My eyes become veiled; my ears sing. I sweat. My entire body shakes. The world has turned a different colour and I am about to bid life adieu.'

Historically speaking, because of its power to disrupt lives and the social order, passion is never in fashion with moralists. They usually think of it as a menace to society.

The Roman philosopher Boethius, who reckoned the route to human happiness lay in the pursuit of wisdom and love of God, saw passion as poison: 'When [Lady Philosophy] saw the muses of Poetry surround my bed, dictating words to accompany my tears, she became angry. "Who," she demanded, her penetrating eyes blazing, "allowed these hysterical whores to approach the sickbed of this man? They have no medicine to ease his pain, only sweet poison to make it worse. These are the women who murder the rich and fertile harvest of Reason with thorns of Passion."'

Down the ages, philosophers, priests and psychologists have begged us — commanded us! — not to let ourselves be overwhelmed by our emotions.

Different religions, civilisations and cultures have tried various forms of rigid control.

In ancient Sparta, *all* expressions of passion were forbidden. Even married people were only permitted to make love in secret and it was as big a scandal to be found in bed with your own spouse as with someone else's. It didn't work of course. What could be sexier than arranging all those secret trysts and rendezvous? As Montaigne said: 'The risk of being caught, the embarrassment of the day after ... that is what makes it so fascinating!'

When all's said and done, we don't really need Passion Police. Some form of well-equipped emotional fire brigade would be much more useful.

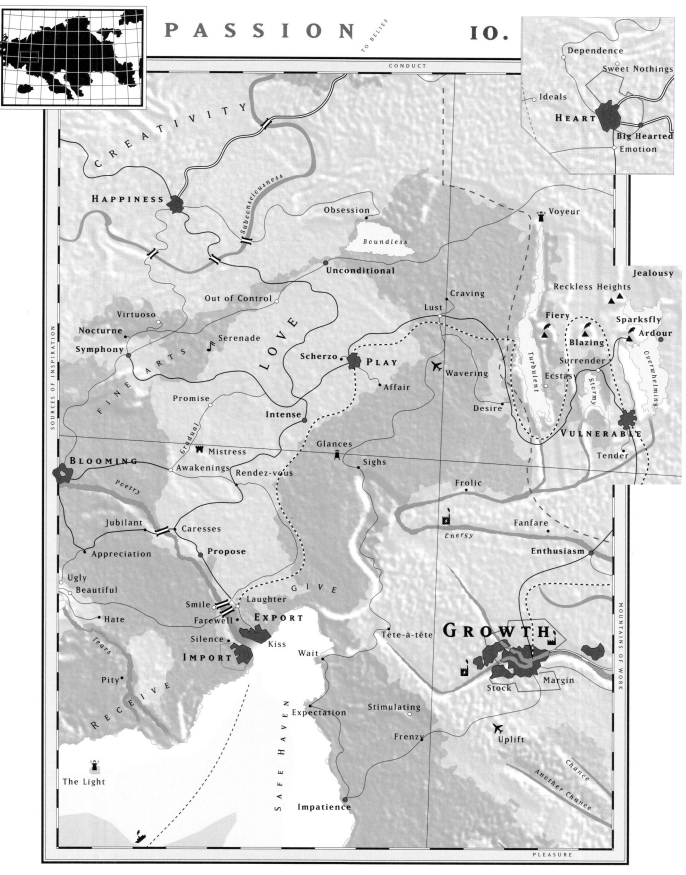

TO BELIEF

CONDUCT

HEART

Dependence
Sweet Nothings
Ideals
Big Hearted
Emotion

Jealousy
Reckless Heights
Fiery
Sparksfly
Ardour
Blazing
Surrender
Turbulent
Ecstasy
Stormy
Overwhelming
VULNERABLE
Tender

CREATIVITY

HAPPINESS

Subconsciousness

Obsession

Boundless

Voyeur

Unconditional

Craving

Lust

Out of Control

Virtuoso
Nocturne
Symphony
Serenade

LOVE

Scherzo
PLAY
Affair
Wavering

Desire

FINE ARTS

Promise
Intense

Gradual

Mistress
Awakenings
Rendez-vous

Glances
Sighs

Frolic

BLOOMING

Poetry

Jubilant
Caresses
Appreciation
Propose
Ugly
Beautiful
Smile
Laughter
Hate
Farewell
EXPORT

GIVE

Fanfare

Enthusiasm

Energy

MOUNTAINS OF WORK

GROWTH

Tête-à-tête

SOURCES OF INSPIRATION

Silence
Kiss
IMPORT
Wait

Stock
Margin

Pity

Tears

RECEIVE

Expectation
Stimulating

SAFE HAVEN

Frenzy
Uplift

The Light

Impatience

Chance

Another Chance

PLEASURE

SCALE
10 20 30 40 50

An old lady can take most of a day to write and send a single postcard to her niece in Littlehampton. It takes her an hour to find the right card, for a start. 'Where did I put my glasses?' That's another hour. Actually writing the card takes up to ninety minutes. There's half an hour to check the address, and the process of making a decision about whether or not to take an umbrella to the postbox can take another twenty minutes. So a task which would take a busy person no more than about three minutes leads to a day of frustration and effort. Thus the British historian and wit, C. Northcote Parkinson, illustrated his theory that 'work expands to fill the time available for its completion'.

Most of us know all about this 'Parkinson's Law'. We yearn for shorter working hours, more days off and longer holidays. We even look forward to our retirement because we know we can – at last – do all the important things we don't have time for now.

Yet when the golden day finally arrives, we are appalled to discover we still don't have time to learn Italian, visit art galleries or give the garden shed a good clean. This is because we spend all morning taking the dog to the vet and there were e-mails to answer – and that took all afternoon. What we used to get done in no time when we were busy people ('between acts', as the French say) now turns out to be a mountain of work. So we still don't have time for the really important stuff.

Meanwhile, over the last decade or so, as people with jobs have discovered, employers (who were a little slow to catch on at first) have applied the principles of Parkinson's Law. Never before have the few people who still have work had so much work to do. Fewer and fewer people do more and more work and where does that leave the rest of the population? Up to their ears in it, that's where – and the garden shed's *still* a mess.

Still, we mustn't grumble, must we? Having work is a privilege and isn't labour essentially noble? Well, not according to Xenophon, the ancient Greek historian, who viewed hard work with contempt: 'Handicrafts ruin the bodies of craftsmen and foremen, forcing them to sit still and live indoors and in some cases to spend the day in front of the fire. And the weakening of the body is accompanied by a serious weakening of the mind. Furthermore, these so-called crafts leaving no time to devote to friend and country, so that those who practise such have a reputation for being wanting in friendship and poor defenders of their homeland.'

The modern-day version of this view might be the line: 'Work is the curse of the drinking classes'. But Xenophon was way ahead of his time in spotting a connection between work and personality. More than 2,200 years went by before Hegel and Marx looked again at the concept. Hegel said (approximately) 'What you do influences who you are and as the other way around is also true.' Marx, in 1844, took the idea that stage further: 'If you are alienated from what you do you are alienated from yourself.' Marx felt that anyone who works for another would be alienated because he would belong to that other person.

This doesn't help us much today. Whenever we feel alienated from our jobs or our colleagues, we don't take the drastic decision to become self-employed. And we don't incite our fellow alienated workers to socialist revolution. No, we go off on a jolly team-building survival weekend in the New Forest. This supposedly enables us to discover ourselves completely and also improves our chances of survival within the company. We just get on with it.

Various factors shape our feelings towards our work at different times of our lives – the pressure and variety of the work itself; the state of our marriage, and so on. When work is a strain, we hate people who seem to work less than we do but earn more than us. We even resent the people who don't need to work or can't work. And we are especially jealous of people who enjoy their work so much it seems to be their hobby.

Contrariwise, when we are happy in our work, earning more seems a little less important and we view the unemployed people with pity and compassion. All of a sudden, our work has become our hobby.

We work too hard and others don't pull their weight. They earn too much and we aren't paid enough. When they fail, some get a golden handshake. Others are made redundant. Some people leap from one exciting job to another while others are stuck in hopeless monotony. Some people spend their lives sending out CVs; others get head-hunted. We survive all this and make it to our retirements. And then we have more mountains of work to look forward to – Parkinson's sort.

Perhaps there is nobility in labour after all.

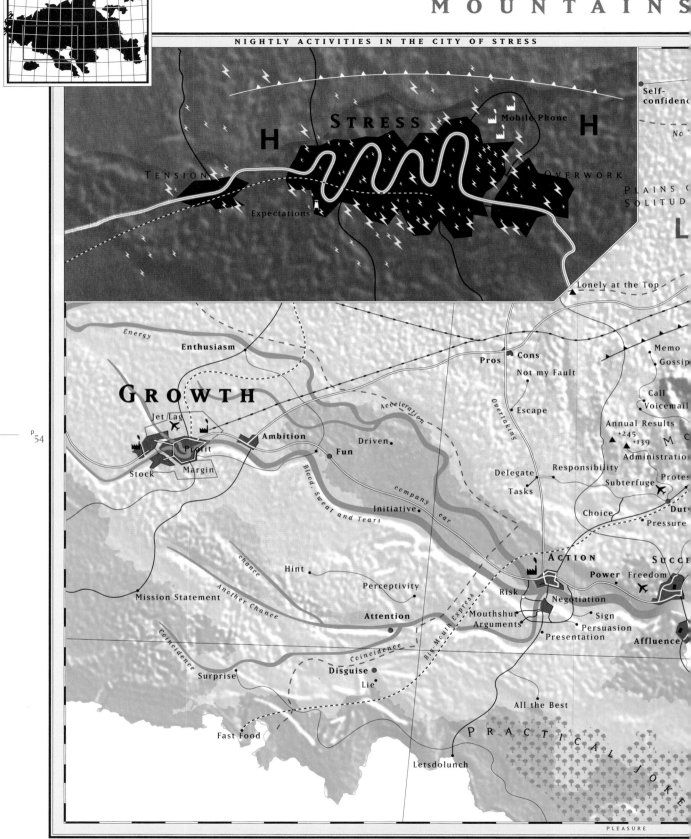

NIGHTLY ACTIVITIES IN THE CITY OF STRESS

H

STRESS

H

TENSION

OVERWORK

Mobile Phone

Expectations

Self-confidenc

No

PLAINS O
SOLITUD

L

Lonely at the Top

Energy

Enthusiasm

Pros   Cons

Not my Fault

Memo
Gossip

GROWTH

Acceleration

Escape

Call
Voicemail

Jet Lag

Overtaking

Annual Results

Profit

Ambition

Driven

+245

+139

M C

Stock

Margin

Fun

Administration

Responsibility

Delegate

Subterfuge

Protes

Tasks

Blood Sweat and Tears

company car

Initiative

Choice

Dut

Pressure

chance

Hint

ACTION

SUCCE

Power   Freedom

Mission Statement

Another Chance

Perceptivity

Risk

Negotiation

Affluence

Coincidence

Attention

Mouthshut
Arguments

Sign

Persuasion

Presentation

Big Mouth Express

Coincidence

Surprise

Disguise

Lie

All the Best

P R A C T I C A L   J O K E

Fast Food

Letsdolunch

PLEASURE

SCALE

10   20   30

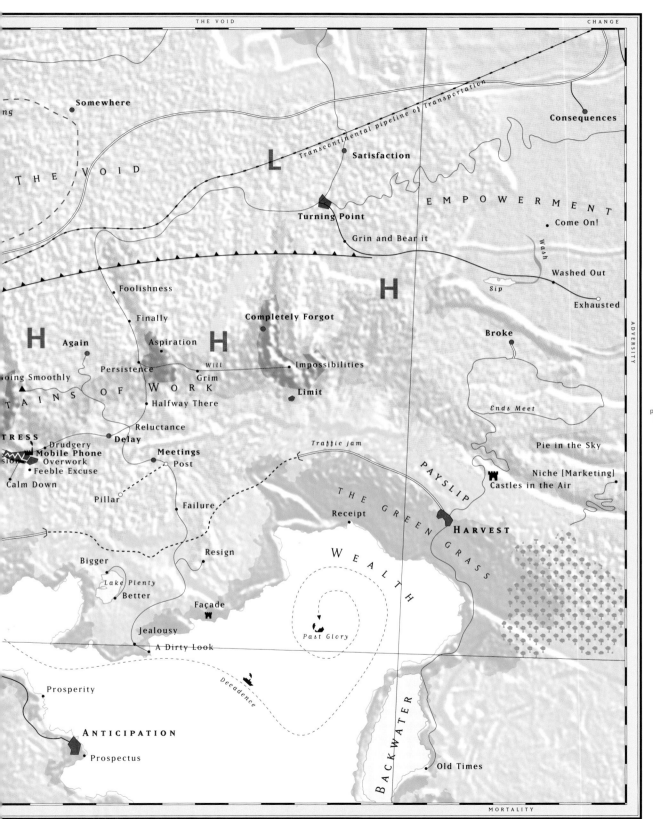

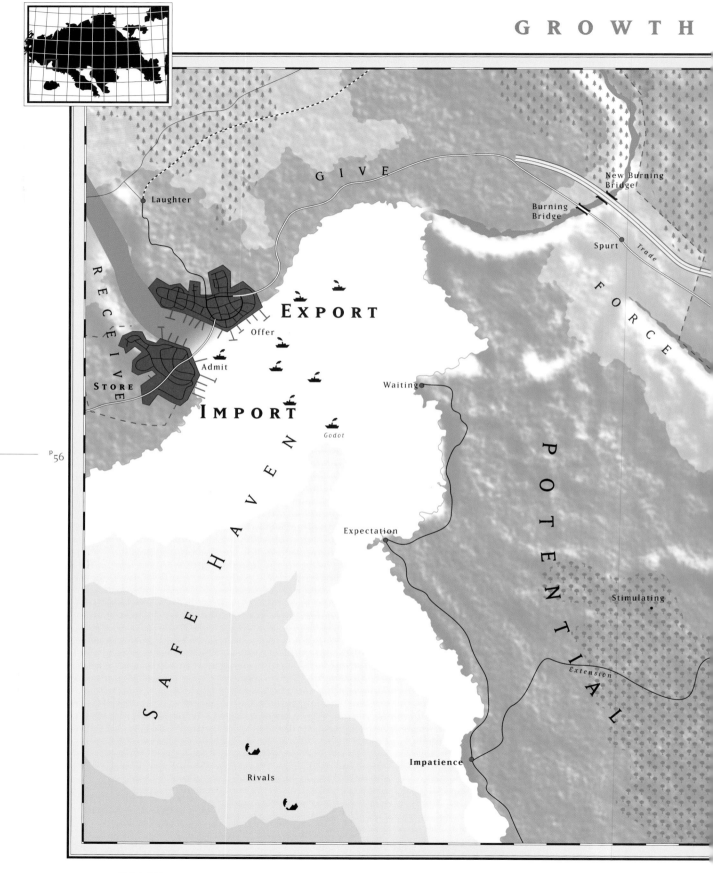

GIVE

New Burning
Bridge

Burning
Bridge

Laughter

Spurt

Trade

FORCE

EXPORT

Offer

RECEIVE

Admit

Waiting

STORE

IMPORT

Godot

SAFE HAVEN

Expectation

POTENTIAL

Stimulating

Rivals

Extension

Impatience

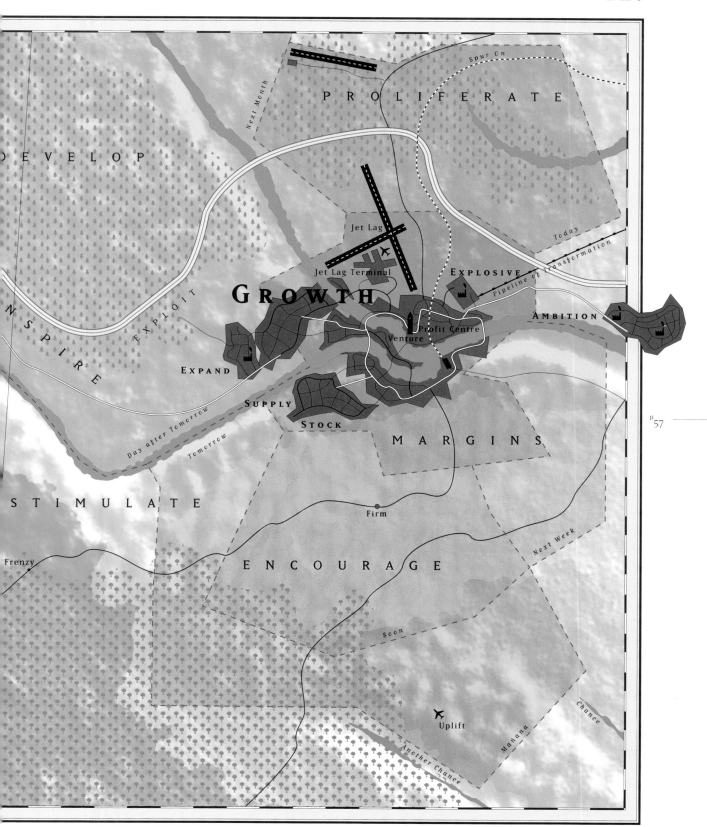

PROLIFERATE

Spur On

DEVELOP

Next Month

Jet Lag

Today

Jet Lag Terminal

EXPLOSIVE

GROWTH

Pipeline of Transformation

INSPIRE

EXPLOIT

AMBITION

Profit Centre

Venture

EXPAND

SUPPLY

Day after Tomorrow

STOCK

Tomorrow

MARGINS

STIMULATE

Firm

Frenzy

ENCOURAGE

Next Week

Soon

Uplift

Mañana

Chance

Another Chance

Doctor: What kind of 'void'?
Boris: An *empty* void.
Doctor: An *empty* void?
Boris: I felt a *full* void a month ago, but it was just something I ate.
Woody Allen, *Love and Death*

Oblomov, the eponymous hero of Ivan Goncharov's great Russian novel, was a sweet-natured, indecisive young nobleman who didn't get out much. Didn't get out at all, in fact. Despite perfect health, he lay in bed all day — every day — contemplating his happy childhood. Nothing could raise him from his torpor until (about 200 pages into the book) his friend Stoltz briefly persuaded him to rejoin society. But Oblomov soon tired of the social whirl. Even when he fell madly in love with a pretty girl called Olga, she provided only a temporary distraction. He soon gave up on her too and went back to bed.

Oblomov is one of the more intriguing characters of world literature and much has been written about him, most of it uncomplimentary. In Russian, the word *oblomovshchina* is still used to refer to the backwardness, inertia, and futility of nineteenth-century Russian society. On the internet, 'Oblomov' is the name of a discussion list for psychologists researching 'academic and general procrastination'.

But some see Oblomov as a 'hidden and heavenly soul'. The German playwright Franz Xaver Kroetz has argued that Oblomov's 'vice' of laziness was, in reality, a virtue. 'I'll show you the life of the mind,' said the terrifying Charlie Meadows at the end of the Hollywood satire *Barton Fink* as his malevolent soul burns down the hotel. But Oblomov's soul and mind were wholly benign. He filled his 'empty' existence with dreams of paradise. Oblomov, in other words, may have been an Eastern-style mystic about a hundred years ahead of his time.

'Nothing will come of nothing,' said King Lear. In *Being and Nothingness*, Jean-Paul Sartre laid out his existentialist philosophy, exploring time, responsibility, reality and appearance and the limits of freedom. Sartre argued that existence was pointless, 'contingent' and absurd. Meanwhile, physicists and mathematicians have begun to ponder the discovery that the Void is one of the essential components of Creation: there seem to be huge amounts of Nothingness (a weird kind of matter with anti-gravity properties) which keep universes separate.

A lot of deep thinking about the Void has come from the East. Feng Shui, ikebana and T'ai Chi are all concerned with achieving harmony. The concept of yin and yang sees empty and full as balancing opposites. The emptier our minds are, the more they can be filled with the wondrous and exalted.

Lao Tze's ancient book of wisdom, *The Te-Tao Ching*, advises:

> *Take emptiness to its utmost limits:*
> *Maintain peace in the middle.*
> *The ten thousand things — side by side they appear:*
> *And through this I see their return.*
> *Things appear in large numbers:*
> *Each returns to its roots.*
> *This is called the peace.*
> *Peace: this means returning to your destination.*
> *Returning to your destination is to be eternal:*
> *Knowing eternity is wisdom:*
> *Not knowing eternity is being wild and reckless:*
> *When you are wild and reckless, your actions will lead to*
> *   misfortune.*

The Void may be a principle of the East, but it has also become fashionable in the West.

Sometimes we don't want to avoid the Void. When someone gives us flowers, it's nice to have an empty vase. Finding an empty train carriage is a stroke of luck; an empty motorway is almost a miracle. Making the first pen strokes in an empty notebook or the first steps in an empty new house are sources of pure delight.

But even though the Void may be a little hip, it remains a lot scary. The truth is that our first instinct when we sense a Void opening within us is to fill it up immediately with frantic action of almost any kind. No one wants to be considered empty and, deep down, we don't really approve of Oblomov.

In *Care of the Soul: A Guide for Cultivating Depth and Sacredness in Everyday Life*, the American writer Thomas Moore warns us not to be tempted to fill this unpleasant sense of Void too quickly. A good Void, he says, can allow us to find our own strength. If we distract ourselves with meaningless activities, we will lose more than we gain.

Oblomov rejected passion and social engagement and achieved fulfilment by lying in bed in his oriental dressing-gown. Did he know something we don't?

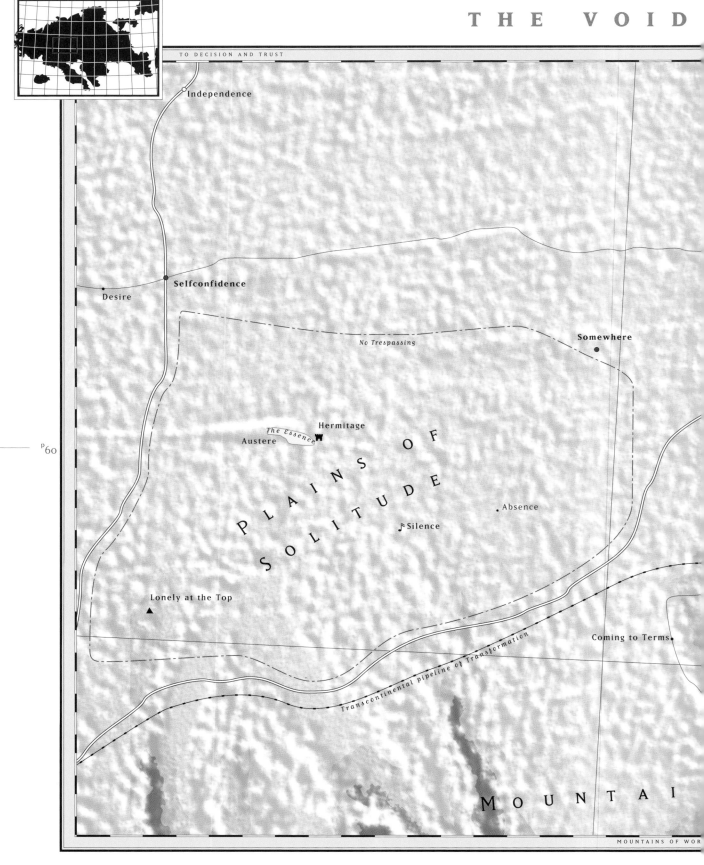

Independence

Desire · Selfconfidence

No Trespassing

Somewhere

Hermitage
The Essence
Austere

PLAINS OF SOLITUDE

· Absence

Silence

Lonely at the Top

Coming to Terms

Transcontinental Pipeline of Transformation

MOUNTAI

MOUNTAINS OF WOR

P60

SCALE

6   12   18   24   30   36

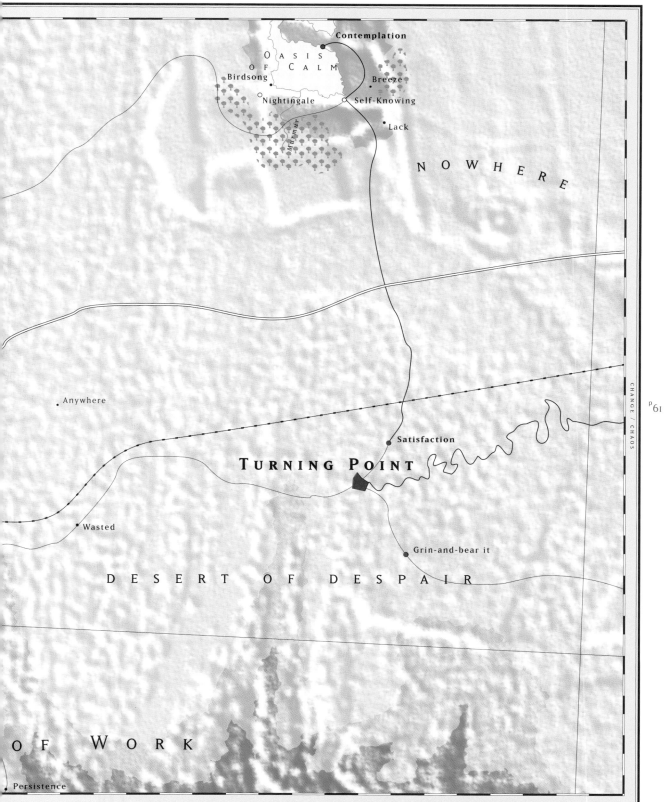

Contemplation

O A S I S
O F   C A L M

Birdsong
○ Nightingale   Breeze
                      ○ Self-Knowing
        Murmur
                       • Lack

N O W H E R E

• Anywhere

Satisfaction

TURNING POINT

• Wasted

• Grin-and-bear it

D E S E R T   O F   D E S P A I R

O F   W O R K

• Persistence

ADVERSITY MAP 14

'I'm singin' in the rain, Just singin' in the rain ...
What a glorious feeling, I'm happy again ...
I'm laughing at clouds, so dark up above ...
The sun's in my heart, and I'm ready for love.'
Arthur Freed and Nacio Herb Brown

'In a dark time, the eye begins to see.'
Theodore Roethke

'I'm very brave generally,' he went on in a low voice:
'only today I happen to have a headache.'
Tweedledum, *Through the Looking Glass* by Lewis Carroll

When the going gets tough, the tough get going, sang Billy Ocean. Moreover, Anaïs Nin remarked: 'Life shrinks or expands in proportion to one's courage.' This doesn't necessarily apply, though, to death-obsessed depressives. In *Annie Hall*, Woody Allen's alter-ego Alvy Singer insists life is divided into two categories – the horrible and the miserable. 'The horrible would be like, um, I don't know, terminal cases, you know, and blind people, crippled. I don't know how they get through life. It's amazing to me, you know, and the miserable is everyone else. That's – that's – so – so – when you go through life – you should be thankful that you're miserable because you're very lucky to be miserable.'

The astonishing Helen Keller never thought of herself as lucky to be miserable. In the first nineteen months of her life, she was a bright and lively infant, but then she was hit by a mysterious viral infection which left her deaf, blind and desperate. 'I cannot remember how I felt when the light went out of my eyes. I suppose I felt it was always night and perhaps I wondered why the day did not come,' she recalled many years later. In her dark, silent world, Helen became uncontrollably wild, expressing her frustration through raging tantrums. When she was nearly seven, her parents hired a teacher for her called Anne Sullivan, herself the survivor of a violent and unhappy childhood. Sullivan was loving and attentive to her new charge. As she later explained: 'I wanted to be loved. I was lonesome – then Helen came into my life. I wanted her to love me and I loved her.'

From the time before her illness, Helen had retained a faint memory of light. She had also made sounds and dimly remembered the word 'wah-wah' for water. One day Sullivan took Helen to a water pump and, as she held the little girl's hands under the flow, traced the word water into her other hand several times. Suddenly, Helen understood that 'water' was the name of the liquid she felt on her hand. She stopped and touched the earth to ask its name. By nightfall, she had learned thirty words in this fashion.

Over the next fifty years, Sullivan devoted herself to Helen. She was her best friend and gateway to the world. Keller learned to read and write. Later she taught herself foreign languages, learned to lip-read by touching people's mouths as they spoke and to speak herself. Her intelligence and passion for learning became the stuff of legend. She insisted on going to college ('It was my right as well as my duty'). Sullivan spelled book after book and lecture after lecture into Helen's hand until she graduated cum laude from Radcliffe College, the first blind-deaf person ever to do so.

For the next fifty years, Keller championed women's and workers' rights and fought for the oppressed and the blind. 'Ignorance and poverty are the causes of much blindness. These are the enemies which destroy the rights of children and workmen, and undermine the health of mankind. These causes must be searched out and abolished.' She wrote thirteen books and was a frequent contributor to magazines and newspapers, writing most often on blindness, deafness, social issues, and women's rights.

Sometimes the most terrifying adversity can trigger courage and determination. In June 1940, when Hitler's blitzkrieg had just crushed France and routed the British army and many neutrals assumed Britain would have to sue for peace or face destruction, Winston Churchill combined defiance with inspiration:

> What General Weygand called the Battle of France is over. I expect that the Battle of Britain is about to begin. Upon this battle depends the survival of Christian civilization. Upon it depends our own British life, and the long continuity of our institutions and our Empire. The whole fury and might of the enemy must very soon be turned on us. Hitler knows that he will have to break us in this Island or lose the war. If we can stand up to him, all Europe may be free and the life of the world may move forward into broad, sunlit uplands. But if we fail, then the whole

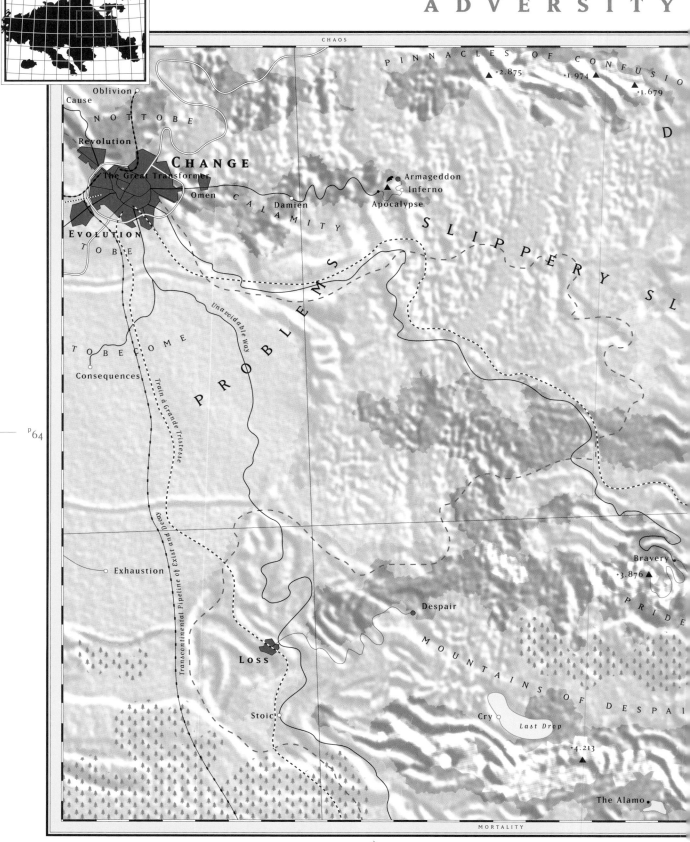

CHAOS

PINNACLES OF CONFUSIO

▲ ·2.875   ▲ ·1.974   ▲ ·1.679

D

Oblivion

Cause

N O T T O B E

Revolution

CHANGE

The Great Transformer

Omen   C A L A M I T Y   Armageddon

Damien   Inferno

Apocalypse

Evolution

T O B E

S L I P P E R Y   S L

T O B E C O M E

Unavoidable Way

P R O B L E M S

Consequences

Train à Grande Tristesse

Transcontinental Pipeline of Exist and Decay

Exhaustion

Bravery

·3.876 ▲

Despair   P R I D E

Loss   M O U N T A I N S   O F   D E S P A I

Stoic   Cry

Last Drop   ·4.213 ▲

The Alamo

MORTALITY

TO MEMORY
AND
DREAMS

Miasma

A D

S L O U G H   O F   D E S P O N D

T R I U M P H

Tall Stories

Relief

Embrace

Adrenalin   •8.826

Impossibubble

Peaks of Euphoria

•4.956

Jan Davis

Climb

Endure

Suffer

Solace   •2.537

Pity

Pessimism

H U M I L I A T I O N

Jeopardy

Possibubble

T R E K

Dogged

Bystander

Last Straw

P E A K S

B I T E   T H E   D U S T

Bruises

Escape

Hunt

L O W   S P I R I T S

Smuggling Route

C O U R A G E

Pass of Heroes

nknown Soldier

Napoleon

Hero

Blinkers

Up the Creek

Attila

Cold Blood

Against the Tide

Q U E S T

C O R N E R

Broken-Winged

F E A R   A N D   T R E M B L E

Quake

Colditz   Cold Sweat

ght

Dark Tunnel (Claustrophobia)

Sweat

world, including the United States, including all that we have known and cared for, will sink into the abyss of a new Dark Age made more sinister, and perhaps more protracted, by the lights of perverted science. Let us therefore brace ourselves to our duties, and so bear ourselves that, if the British Empire and its Commonwealth last for a thousand years, men will still say, "This was their finest hour."

'Courage is a special kind of knowledge: the knowledge of how to fear what ought to be feared and how not to fear what ought not to be feared,' said David Ben-Gurion. Ernest Hemingway defined courage as 'grace under pressure'.

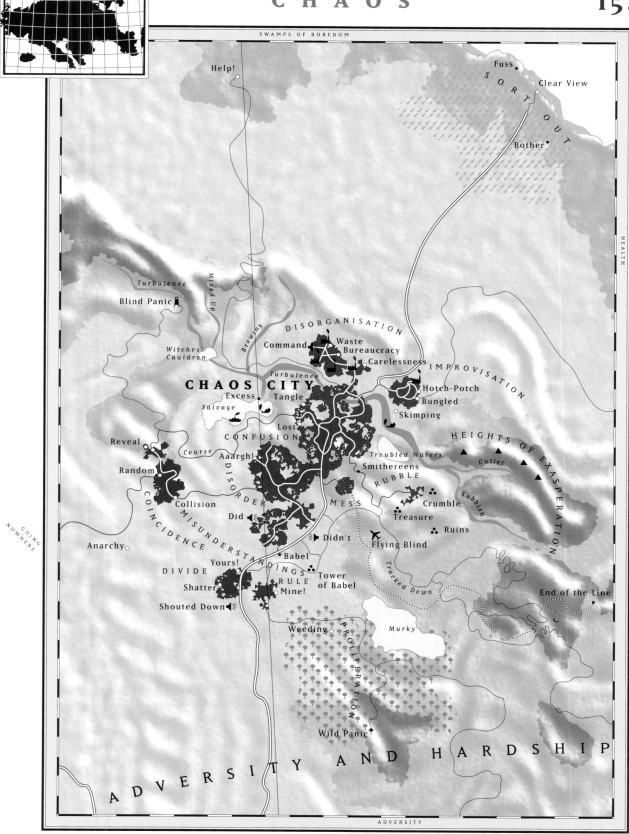

SWAMPS OF BOREDOM

Fuss •
Clear View

SORT OUT

Bother •

Help! ○

HEALTH

Turbulence
Blind Panic ■

Mixed Up

Brewing

Witches'
Cauldron

DISORGANISATION

Command ■
Waste
Bureaucracy
Carelessness

IMPROVISATION

Hotch-Potch ○
Bungled
Skimping •

CHAOS CITY

Turbulence
Excess ○ Tangle
Salvage

Lost
CONFUSION

Troubled Waters

HEIGHTS OF EXASPERATION

Outlet ▲ ▲ ▲ ▲

Reveal ○

Course

Aaargh! ■

Smithereens •

RUBBLE

Rubbish

Random ○

DISORDER

Crumble

Collision

Did ◄

MESS

Treasure

Ruins

Anarchy ○

MISUNDERSTANDINGS

Didn't ►

Flying Blind

End of the Line

COINCIDENCE

Babel •

Yours!

DIVIDE

RULE
Mine!

Tower
of Babel

Shatter

Tracked Down

GOING
NOWHERE

Shouted Down ◄

PROLIFERATION

Weeding ○

Murky

Wild Panic •

A D V E R S I T Y   A N D   H A R D S H I P

ADVERSITY

P67

SCALE
0 1 2

TO CHANGE

SCALE
10 20 30 40 50

'The only thing we have to fear is fear itself.'
Franklin D. Roosevelt

'If at first you don't succeed, try again. Then quit. There's no use being a damn fool about it.'
W.C. Fields

Parachutists do it. Mountain climbers sometimes do it without meaning to. And educated bungee-jumpers do it all the time. (But fleas never do.) As the Cole Porter song doesn't quite go: let's fall from a very high place with a genuine risk of death or injury.

Even for the powerful, pushing physical and psychological limits can be thrilling. As a twenty-year-old US Navy aviator on the aircraft carrier San Jacinto, the future president George Bush had bailed out of his burning torpedo bomber. Fifty-two years later, the by-now former president Bush bailed out again — leaping from the back of a small white plane 12,500 feet above the Arizona Desert. He plunged in freefall for a few seconds before pulling the rip cord and floating to earth where he was greeted by relieved security men. Three years later, Bush celebrated his seventy-fifth birthday in similar fashion. 'It's a euphoric high,' he explained. 'You just feel wonderful. We were rolling around in the sky, unlike the first jump, and it was heaven. It was just exhilarating.'

As the former president skydived, he was filmed by a legendary stunt cameraman called Tom Sanders. Three years after the Arizona jump, Sanders found himself amid the stunning beauty of the Yosemite National Park in California filming another parachutist, his wife Jan Davis, as she BASE-jumped from the top of a 3,600-foot granite cliff called El Capitan. BASE-jumping is like normal parachute jumping, only more dangerous. 'To put your life in danger from time to time ... breeds a saneness in dealing with day-to-day trivialities,' said Nevil Shute. Or as a colleague of Tom and Jan explained: 'Have you ever looked over the edge of a tall building or a cliff and wondered what it would be like to jump off? I wondered and now I know what it's like: You're dead and all of a sudden you're alive again.'

Jan Davis had performed more than 3,000 sky-dives and 70 BASE-jumps and was the first woman to leap from the world's tallest waterfall, Angel Falls in Venezuela. She had discovered the pleasure of jumping after the death of her first husband: 'I needed something to focus all my attention on, kind of a grief therapy,' she explained later. 'I soon became addicted and went hard core. I feel very lucky now to make my living from something I have such passion for. I truly believe it's not because things are difficult that we don't dare; it's because we do not dare that they are difficult.'

Her Yosemite leap was part of a political protest against park authorities who had banned BASE-jumping for being too dangerous. As she threw herself from the granite cliff, she was dressed in symbolic prisoner's stripes. Because she was to be arrested and her equipment confiscated, she used a borrowed parachute. 'As far as I could tell, she looked as if she had a good, stable exit,' Sanders said later. 'There was never any tumbling. And she just continued to fall, and fall, and fall. But when she continued to fall, and once I saw the trees come into frame, I knew it was too late.' As his wife hit the ground, eye-witnesses saw the grief-stricken Sanders collapse on to his camera.

'Life is about action and passion, and you truly can't begin to live life until you overcome your fear of dying,' Jan Davis had said, and her death failed to persuade park authorities or her fellow BASE-jumpers to change their minds about the sport. Three weeks after the tragedy, Sanders and Jan's colleagues and friends held a memorial service. There was sky-jumping, the scattering of her ashes from a plane and, at sunset, a mass simulta-neous parachute jump involving more than 100 people jumping from four planes.

Humans have always had a deep need to 'push the outside of the envelope', as the test pilots and astronauts of Tom Wolfe's *The Right Stuff* put it. 'Whether we call it sacrifice, or poetry, or adventure, it is always the same voice that calls,' said Antoine de Saint-Exupéry. Somewhere along the line, defying death can become a compulsion. The American mountaineer Jim Wickwire, who conquered K2 and wrote a book called *Addicted to Danger*, said: 'You get into a tight situation, you get hurt; a friend gets killed, and you think you're going to stop climbing. But, after a few weeks at home, you start planning your next climb.'

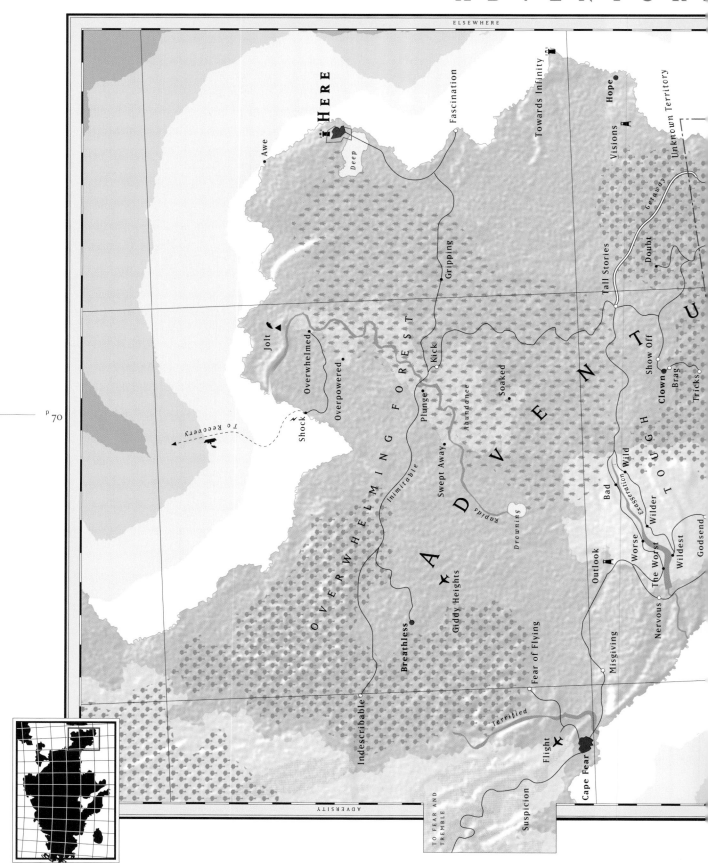

ELSEWHERE

HERE

Awe

Deep

Fascination

Towards Infinity

Hope

Visions

Unknown Territory

Getaway

Gripping

Tall Stories

Doubt

Jolt

Overwhelmed

Overpowered

O V E R W H E L M I N G   F O R E S T

Kick

Soaked

A D V E N T

Show Off

Brag

Clown

Tricks

To Recovery

Shock

Inimitable

Plunge

Abundance

Swept Away

Rapids

Drowning

Bad

Wild

Exaggeration

Wilder

T O U G H

Godsend

Breathless

Giddy Heights

Worse

The Worst

Wildest

Indescribable

Fear of Flying

Outlook

Misgiving

Nervous

Terrified

Flight

Cape Fear

Suspicion

TO FEAR AND TREMBLE

ADVERSITY

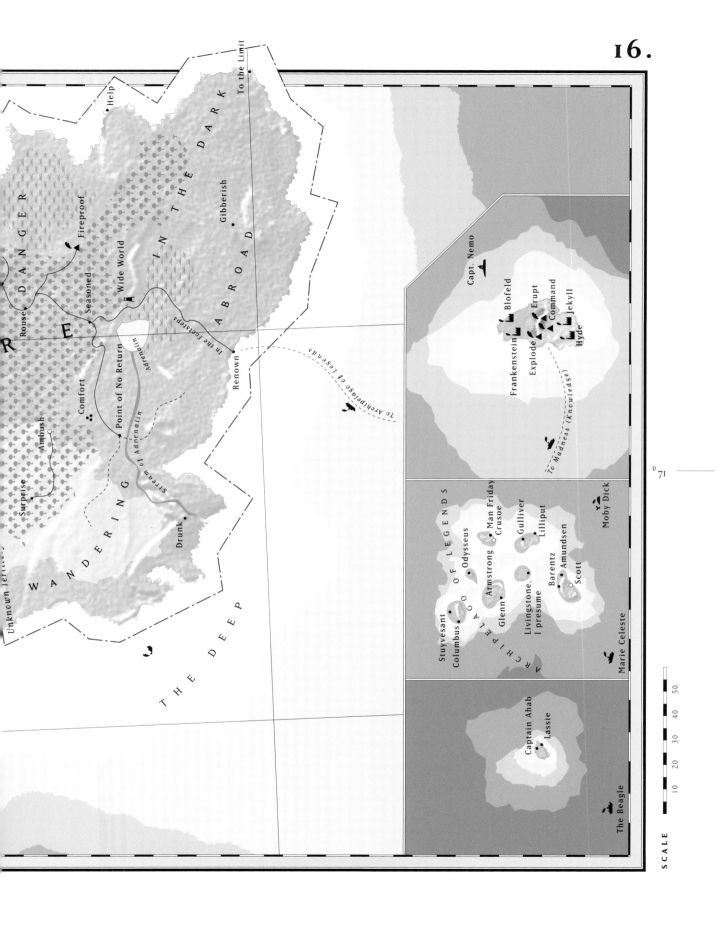

DANGER

Rouse •

Fireproof

Seasoned

Wide World

Help •

IN THE DARK

Gibberish •

Comfort

ABROAD

FIRE

Ambush

Point of No Return

In the Footsteps

Surprise

Renown •

Stream of Adrenalin

Adrenalin

Unknown Territory

WANDERING

Drunk •

To the Limit

To Archipelago of Legends

THE DEEP

Capt. Nemo

Blofeld

Erupt

Command

Frankenstein

Explode

Jekyll

Hyde

To Madness (Knowledge)

ARCHIPELAGO OF LEGENDS

Stuyvesant

Columbus •

Odysseus

Man Friday

Crusoe

Armstrong

Gulliver

Glenn

Lilliput

Livingstone, I presume

Barentz

Amundsen

Scott

Moby Dick

Marie Celeste

Captain Ahab

Lassie

The Beagle

SCALE

10   20   30   40   50

> *'A woman drove me to drink, and I'll be a son-of-a-gun but I never even wrote to thank her.'*
> W.C. Fields

Few obscure historical figures loved food as much as the ill-fated Roman Emperor Vitellius. According to his enemies, Vitellius used to enjoy at least four big meals (and a drunken revel) every day. He was also in the habit of vomiting copiously to keep himself hungry and would even grab food-offerings at religious ceremonies or scoff left-overs from roadside taverns when he travelled. At one gargantuan meal for which the phrase 'huge banquet' seems a feeble understatement, his brother served up 2,000 fishes and 7,000 birds for the emperor. Another feast involved a ginormous dish known as 'Minerva's Shield' in which 'were tossed together the livers of charfish, the brains of pheasants and peacocks, with the tongues of flamingos and the entrails of lampreys, which had been brought in ships of war as far as from the Carpathian Sea and the Spanish Straits' (Suetonius). It may have been fun while it lasted, but Vitellius is remembered, if at all, as a greedy, cruel tyrant. When he was overthrown after less than a year in power, he tried to escape by disguising himself in dirty clothing but he was captured, dragged half-naked to the Forum, tortured and thrown into the Tiber. A dishonourable end for an emperor. Tacitus's verdict: 'Vitellius with his sensuality and gluttony was his own enemy.'

Another unforgettable big man with what Iggy Pop calls 'a lust for life' (for food anyway) is Mr Creosote from the French restaurant in Monty Python's *Meaning of Life*:

Maître d': Ah, good afternoon, sir, and how are we today?
Mr Creosote: Better.
Maître d': Better?
Mr Creosote: Better get a bucket ...
(Once Mr Creosote has finished throwing up into the bucket, the waiter tempts him with 'very delicate, very subtle' delicacies: jugged hare (with a sauce made of truffles, anchovies, Grand Marnier, bacon and cream), moules marinières, pâté de foie gras, beluga caviare, eggs Benedict, leek tart, frog's legs amandine, quail's eggs on a bed of pureed mushroom ...)
Mr Creosote: I'll have the lot.
Maître d': A wise choice, Monsieur. And now, how would you like it served? All, uh, mixed up togezer in a bucket?
Mr Creosote: Yeah ... with the eggs on top.
Maître d': But of course ...

It surely signifies something or other that the word 'food' rhymes much more convincingly with 'rude', 'nude' and 'lewd' than it ever does with 'good', 'understood' or 'sainthood'. Moreover, gluttony, famously, is one of the seven deadly sins. But foodie-ness can be — and often is — next to godliness.

In literature and film, food is seldom just for eating. It is charged with emotional, spiritual or character significance. 'Leave the gun; take the cannoli,' says Clemenza in *The Godfather*. Michael Ondaatje's *Anil's Ghost* alludes to the sublime possibilities of food-giving trees: 'It was legendary that every Tamil home in Jaffna Peninsula had three trees in the garden. A mango tree, a murunga tree, and the pomegranate. Murunga leaves were cooked in crab curries to neutralise poisons, pomegranate leaves were soaked in water for the care of eyes and the fruit eaten to aid digestion.' Food is a metaphor for life in *Eat Drink Man Woman*. In $9^1/_2$ *Weeks*, the contents of a fridge become a sophisticated sex toy.

Yet food — as art and a sublime spiritual force for healing and redemption — has never seemed as beautiful as in Karen Blixen's story *Babette's Feast*. In a bleak little Scandinavian village two devoted daughters of a pastor live with Babette, a mysterious French housekeeper. The once-beautiful and gifted daughters have followed their father's puritanical teachings, eschewing all sensual pleasures and devoting themselves instead to the pastor and, later, his ageing, bickering disciples. Food in this God-fearing community is as plain and tasteless as possible: salted fish, dry bread, water, are luxury enough. When Babette wins a small fortune in a French lottery, she cooks a meal celebrating the Pastor's life. Not wishing to appear ungrateful, the congregants swear to 'cleanse our tongues of all taste and purify them of all delight or disgust of the senses, keeping and preserving them for the higher things of praise and thanksgiving'. But the meal, which evokes the Last Supper, is sublime. The blinis Demidof, *cailles en sarcophages*, turtle soup, Amontillado, Veuve Clicquot 1860, grapes, peaches, fresh figs and the other ingredients brought at great expense from Paris combine to generate a state of grace. Babette turns out to have been the greatest chef in Paris, once cook at the Café Anglais, and a supreme artist. She has blown her winnings on the single meal, but seemingly healed a lifetime of regret and self-sacrifice. Over the course of the evening, the congregants kiss and make up and the daughters are redeemed. 'Mercy and Truth have met together. Righteousness and bliss shall kiss,' says the ageing General Lowenhielm, who, as a young hussar, was rejected by one of the daughters, Martine, even though they both loved each other. He tells her:

> 'I have been with you every day of my life. You know, do you not, that it has been so?'
> 'Yes,' says Martine. 'I know that it has been so.'
> 'And,' he continued, 'I shall be with you every day that is left to me. Every evening I shall sit down, if not in the flesh, which means nothing, in spirit, which is all, to dine with you just like tonight. For tonight I have learned, dear sister, that in this world everything is possible.'

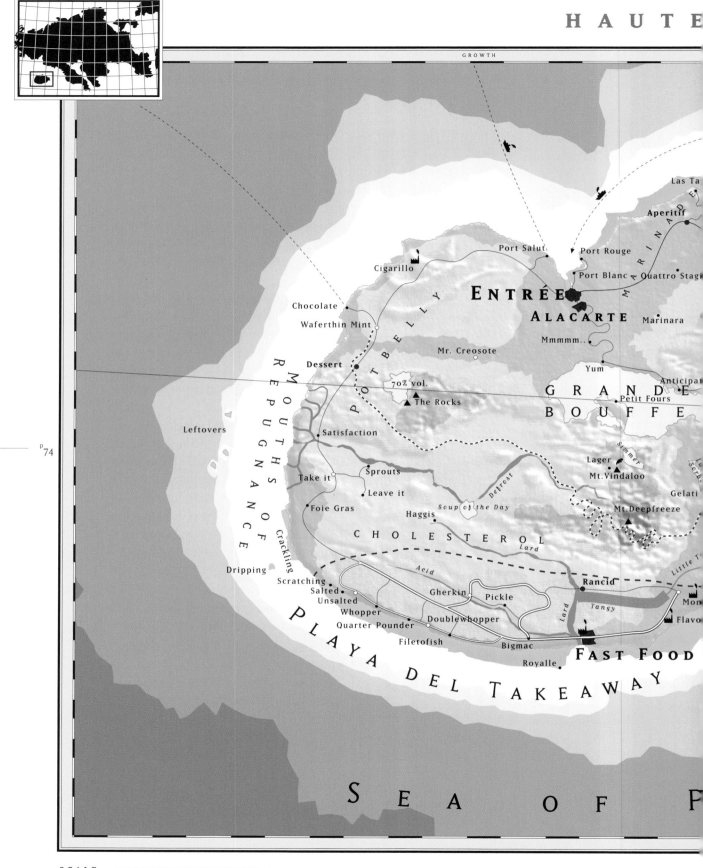

GROWTH

Las Ta

Aperitif

MARINADE

Port Salut
Port Rouge

Cigarillo
Port Blanc Quattro Stag

ENTRÉE
Chocolate
ALACARTE Marinara

Waferthin Mint
Mmmmm..

POTBELLY

Mr. Creosote
Yum
Dessert

Anticipa

M 70% vol. **GRANDE**
O ▲ **BOUFFE**
U ▲ The Rocks
T Petit Fours
H
S Leftovers
O
F Satisfaction Lager Summer

R Mt.Vindaloo ▲
E Sprouts
P Take it Gelati
U
G Leave it Mt.Deepfreeze ▲
N Foie Gras
A Defrost
N
C Haggis Soup of the Day
E Crackling CHOLESTEROL
Lard

Dripping Acid Rancid Mon
Scratching
Salted Gherkin Pickle Tangy Flavo
Unsalted Lard
Whopper Doublewhopper
Quarter Pounder
Filetofish Bigmac **FAST FOOD**
Royalle

PLAYA DEL TAKEAWAY

S E A   O F   P

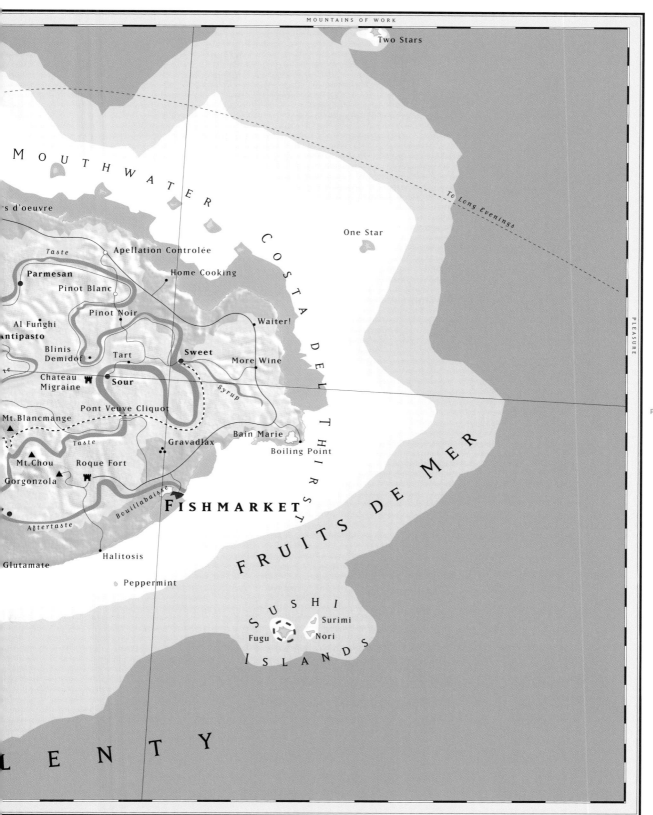

MOUNTAINS OF WORK

Two Stars

To Long Evenings

M O U T H W A T E R

s d'oeuvre

One Star

C O S T A   D E L   T H I R S T

Taste

Apellation Controlée

Parmesan

Home Cooking

Pinot Blanc

Pinot Noir

Al Funghi

Waiter!

ntipasto

Blinis
Demidof

Sweet

Tart

More Wine

Chateau
Migraine

Sour

Syrup

Pont Veuve Cliquot

Mt.Blancmange

Bain Marie

Taste

Gravadlax

Boiling Point

Mt.Chou

Roque Fort

Gorgonzola

F R U I T S   D E   M E R

Bouillabaisse

FISHMARKET

Aftertaste

Glutamate

Halitosis

Peppermint

S U S H I

Surimi

Fugu

Nori

I S L A N D S

L E N T Y

PLEASURE

Man:	*You were wonderful tonight.*
Mae West:	*I'm always wonderful at night.*
Man:	*Tonight I thought you were especially good.*
Mae West:	*When I'm good I'm very good, but when I'm bad I'm better.*
Man:	*If I could only trust you ...*
Mae West:	*You can — hundreds have.*

A friend of Jimi Hendrix received a call from the rock legend late one night. 'Come right over,' pleaded Hendrix, sounding panicky. 'I need help fast.' The friend rushed to his jeep and raced the eight miles to the star's secluded mansion in Woodstock. When he arrived, the cook told him Hendrix was upstairs in his bedroom, so the friend raced up, taking two stairs at a time, and burst into the room. Hendrix was lying spread-eagled in the middle of his huge bed, surrounded and overwhelmed by six or seven naked girls. He looked up and asked: 'You a friend?'
'Yes.'
'Do me a favour.'
'Anything.'
'Take your clothes off and join me.'

Hendrix was the greatest of all rock guitarists and a living embodiment both of Mae West's line: 'too much of a good thing can be wonderful,' and Ian Dury's lyric: 'Sex and drugs and rock and roll / Is all my brain and body need / Sex and drugs and rock and roll / Are very good indeed.' Living embodiment, that is, until he choked to death in desperate, murky, drug-assisted circumstances in September 1970. The creator of febrile music which still has the power to inspire and astonish was gone at twenty-seven.

Few milieux in human history have been as creative, recklessly experimental or as single-mindedly dedicated to hedonism as the sixties musical underground. 'If you can remember the sixties you weren't there,' as Robin Williams said. But a terrifying price was paid for the fun. Among the leading figures of the counter-culture in the sixties the casualty rate — dead, wounded or missing in action — was akin to that of an RAF squadron during the Battle of Britain. One of the epicentres of excess and excitement was the New York nightclub Max's Kansas City, hangout for the likes of Allen Ginsberg and William S. Burroughs, Roy Lichtenstein and Andy Warhol, Bob Dylan, Mick Jagger, Jim Morrison, David Bowie, Janis Joplin and the Velvet Underground. Some of the denizens of Max's were immortalised in Lou Reed's song 'Walk on the Wild Side'. But Reed later recalled: 'Few of the regulars lived long enough to be a nostalgic memory ... A young, reckless, night-time bunch we were. The dark brigade who never saw the sun.'

Such a fine line between pleasure and destruction. In the elegant black comedy, *La Grande Bouffe*, a group of wealthy middle-aged men retire to a Paris villa, where they indulge themselves in carnal pleasures until they die in a nihilistic blow-out of orgiastic over-indulgence.

And pleasure and pain have always had much more in common than their first letters. 'Pleasure only starts once the worm has got into the fruit. To become delightful, happiness must be tainted with poison,' said Georges Bataille, French documenter of sexual excess and author of books like *The Story of the Eye*, *Literature and Evil* and *L'Érotisme*. Or, as another Frenchman, that dedicated follower of passion, the Marquis de Sade, put it: 'Happiness lies only in that which excites, and the only thing that excites is crime ... I have supported my deviations with reasons; I did not stop at mere doubt; I have vanquished, I have uprooted, I have destroyed everything in my heart that might have interfered with my pleasure.'

Aristotle said: 'The aim of the wise is not to secure pleasure, but to avoid pain.' But when Hendrix sings: 'Scuse me while I kiss the sky ...' how many such 'wise men' even know what he is talking about? 'It's true I spent all my money on booze, women and gambling,' said the glorious footballer and Elvis-impersonator Frank Worthington. 'But at least I didn't waste it.'

But there are gentler and less expensive routes to a good time. The Greek philosopher Epicurus, whose name is a byword for pleasure-seeking, actually argued for moderation: 'It is not possible to enjoy if one does not practise prudence in one's pleasures.' His predecessor, the hedonist Aristippus, urged us to take pleasure in the moment.

Our senses provide intense but simple pleasures every day, if only we paid attention to them: a wonderful sunset, beautiful music, a glorious meal; a lover's caress. Playwright Dennis Potter, in his last television interview as he was dying of cancer, spoke of the extraordinary intensity of his perceptions: 'Below my window in Ross ... the blossom is out now. It's a plum tree, it looks like apple blossom but it's white, and, looking at it through the window when I'm writing, I see it's the whitest, frothiest, blossomest blossom there ever could be, and I can see it. Things are both more trivial than they ever were and more important than they ever were, and the difference between trivial and important doesn't seem to matter. But the "nowness" of everything is wondrous.'

You don't have to be dying to notice beauty, but it seems to help.

MOUNTAINS OF WORK

Surprise

Disguise

Radiant

So What?

P R A C T I C A L   J O K E S

Reckless

Hilarious

Cheerful

Fast Food

Jolly

Sparkle

Cheer

Bubbling

Ha-Harbour

Let's do Lunch

Laughter

Day Out

Twinkling Eyes

Day Out at the Seaside

Wink

Run Riot

Brilliant

Amazing

Lustre

Breathl

Ovation

Motion

Apellation Controlée

Wonder

Discove

Waiter!

To Haute Cuisine

More Wine

Intir

Sparks

Hangover

Hammock

Whisper

To Playa del Takeaway

S E A

Sult

O F

Rock-a-Bye

Rocking

P L E N T Y

HAUTE CUISINE

BEAMIN

A Wonderful Journey

Imperturbable

p78

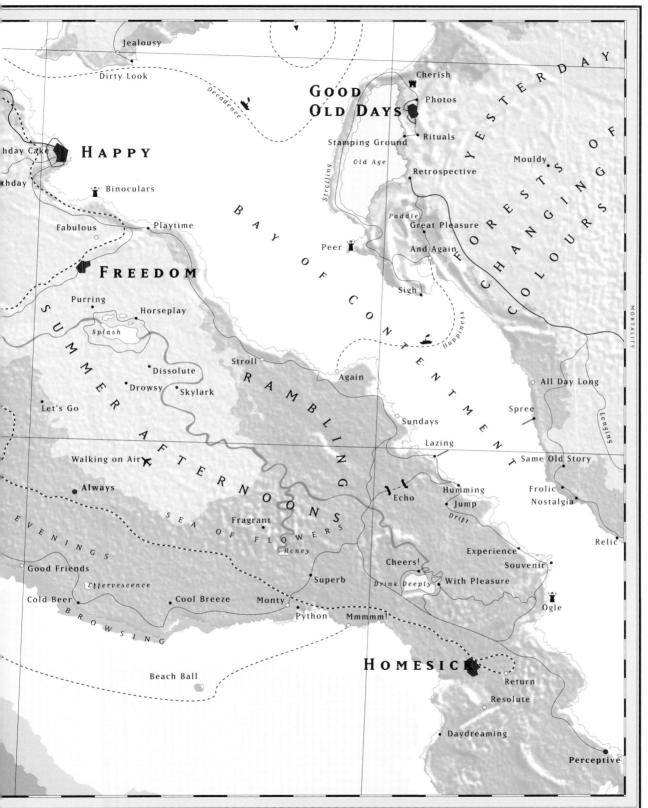

Jealousy

Dirty Look

Decadence

GOOD OLD DAYS

Cherish

Photos

Rituals

Y E S T E R D A Y

hday Cake

HAPPY

Mouldy

Stamping Ground

Old Age

Retrospective

F O R E S T S   O F   C H A N G I N G   O F   C O L O U R S

hday

Binoculars

Fabulous

Playtime

B A Y

Paddle

Great Pleasure

FREEDOM

Peer

And Again

Purring

O F

Sigh

Horseplay

Splash

All Day Long

S U M M E R

Dissolute

Stroll

C O N T E N T M E N T

Spree

L o n g i n g

Let's Go

Drowsy

Skylark

Again

Sundays

A F T E R N O O N S

R A M B L I N G

Lazing

Same Old Story

Walking on Air

M O R T A L I T Y

Always

Humming

Jump

Frolic

Nostalgia

E V E N I N G S

S E A   O F

Fragrant

F L O W E R S

Drift

Echo

Experience

Relic

Honey

Cheers!

Souvenir

Good Friends

Superb

Drink Deeply

With Pleasure

Effervescence

Cold Beer

Cool Breeze

Monty

Ogle

B R O W S I N G

Python

Mmmmm!

Beach Ball

HOMESICK

Return

Resolute

Daydreaming

Perceptive

'If the world were perfect, it wouldn't be.'
Yogi Berra

*'Become a student of change. It is the only thing that will remain
constant.'*
Anthony J. D'Angelo

The philosopher William James was amazed and enchanted when he first visited the
Chautauqua Institution, a fabled New York spiritual holiday resort and education centre
– a 'middle-class paradise' – which thrived in the late nineteenth century. 'The moment
you enter this holy domain, you feel the atmosphere of success,' he wrote admiringly.
'All around, you can feel modesty and diligence, intelligence and goodness, and neat-
ness and excellence, prosperity and cheerfulness.' James went to Chautauqua for a day,
but ended up staying a week, 'enchanted by the charm and convenience of it all, by this
middle-class paradise, without sin, victims, a stain or a tear.' He felt he had stumbled
into Utopia. The place was teeming with the nicest people. There were schools and
sports facilities of every kind, beautiful music was provided by a 700-voice choir in the
world's most perfect open-air auditorium. 'There are no contagious diseases, poverty,
drunkenness, crime or police and you will find culture and friendliness. Everything is
cheap and everybody is the equal of everyone else. You will find here the best of everything mankind has strived for in the name of civilisation and what it has fought and bled
for over the centuries.'

Chautauqua was, in a word, perfect. And James rapidly grew to hate it. By the time he left,
he ached for something primal, urgent and vivid. 'Give me back the large worldly jungle
with all its sins and suffering, where there are peaks and valleys, the beast and high
ideals, the splendour of all that is terrible and infinite. There you will find endlessly
more hope and help than on this level of deadly mediocrity.'

We think we yearn for the highest ideals, for 'happiness'. And we like the idea of striving
for some distant promised land. Yet whenever we reach one, it fails to satisfy. As
Robert Louis Stevenson put it: 'To travel hopefully is a better thing than to arrive, and
the true success is to labour.' We want the struggle and excitement of striving. We
need to be surprised and challenged constantly. We need blood, sweat 'n' tears, for as
soon as we've achieved our goal we are hungry for the next challenge.

We are hopelessly restless creatures, adrenalin junkies who crave ever more vivid stimuli.

As children, every day seemed filled with the wonder and joy of what we saw and experi-
enced. Little by little we discovered the world as it unfolded before our eyes. Actually
it was not the world that was fresh, but our experience of it and the intensity with
which we paid attention to it. For a child, clouds, thunder, a shadow, the ladybird that

lands on a hand, are thrilling. As we grow older, we pay less attention to the present and more to striving towards distant goals. The wonder of daily life disappears because we've seen it all before. We are no longer moved by a stranger's smile, the sun travelling across the sky, or how a clothespeg works.

An ascetic was meditating in a cave when a mouse crept inside and started nibbling his sandal.
The ascetic was irritated and opened his eyes.
'Why are you disturbing my meditation?' he asked fiercely.
'I'm hungry,' squeaked the mouse.
'Go away, foolish mouse!' said the ascetic. 'I'm looking for unity with God. How dare you disturb me?'
'How can you hope to unite with God,' replied the mouse, 'when you cannot even see eye to eye with me?'

Searching for orchids, we miss the daisies. We are so used to focusing on the Future, the New, the Important and the Valuable, that everything that is ordinary and natural escapes our attention.

A man once asked the Zen master Ikkyu to write down some words of his deepest wisdom.
Ikkyu wrote down a single word: 'Attention.'
'Could you add something to that?' asked the man.
Ikkyu wrote down: 'Attention. Attention.'
The man was still not satisfied and said he could find little wisdom in this.
So Ikkyu wrote: 'Attention. Attention. Attention.'
'But what does attention mean?' the man asked finally.
'Attention means attention,' said Ikkyu.

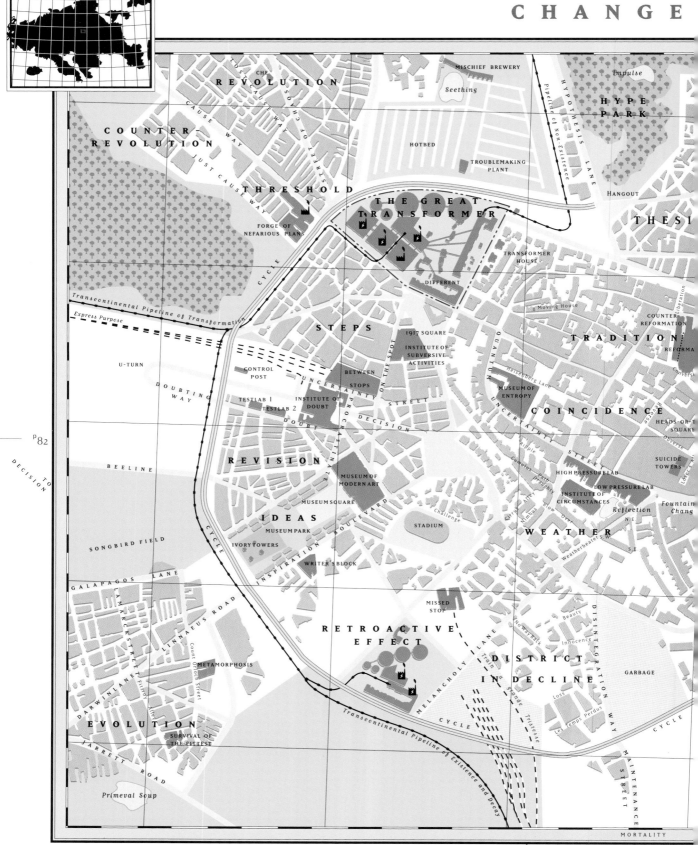

REVOLUTION

CHE

Seething

MISCHIEF BREWERY

Impulse

HYPE
PARK

COUNTER-
REVOLUTION

HOTBED

TROUBLEMAKING
PLANT

Hangout

THRESHOLD

THESI

THE GREAT
TRANSFORMER

FORGE OF
NEFARIOUS PLANS

TRANSFORMER
HOUSE

Moving House

COUNTER-
REFORMATION

DIFFERENT

Express Purpose

STEPS

1917 SQUARE

INSTITUTE OF
SUBVERSIVE
ACTIVITIES

Herrenberg Lane

MUSEUM OF
ENTROPY

TRADITION

REFORMA

Convers

Transcontinental Pipeline of Transformation

U-TURN

CONTROL
POST

BETWEEN
STOPS

COINCIDENCE

HEADS-OR-T
SQUARE

DOUBTING
WAY

TESTLAB 1
TESTLAB 2

INSTITUTE OF
DOUBT

SUICIDE
TOWERS

P82

BEELINE

REVISION

MUSEUM OF
MODERN ART

HIGH PRESSURE LAB

LOW PRESSURE LAB

INSTITUTE OF
CIRCUMSTANCES

Reflection

Fountain
Chang

TO
DECISION

MUSEUM SQUARE

Challenge

IDEAS

MUSEUM PARK

STADIUM

WEATHER

SONGBIRD FIELD

IVORY TOWERS

WRITER'S BLOCK

Weatherbeaters

GALAPAGOS LANE

MISSED
STOP

Beauty

DISTRICT

DISINTEGRATION WAY

Innocence

METAMORPHOSIS

RETROACTIVE
EFFECT

IN DECLINE

GARBAGE

EVOLUTION

SURVIVAL OF
THE FITTEST

Loss

Transcontinental Pipeline of Existence and Decay

MAINTENANCE STREET

Primeval Soup

MORTALITY

TO BE AND
NOT TO BE

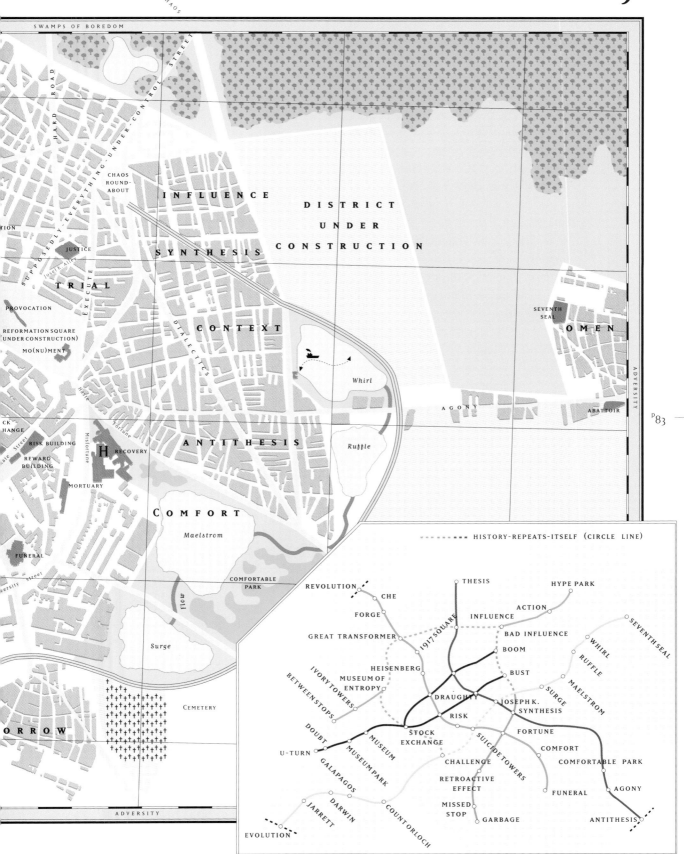

MORTALITY

MAP 20

The opposite of life is not death; the opposite of life is time
Title of sculpture by Morris Graves

'I don't want to achieve immortality through my work. I want to achieve it through not dying,' said Woody Allen. Strangely, though, those who do live for ever tell us that immortality is a lot less fun than it looks. Vampires, for example, have a rotten time. No real friends; chronic allergies, a very limited diet, depression, mood swings ...

As Bram Stoker's Dracula put it: 'I seek not gaiety nor mirth, not the bright voluptuousness of much sunshine and sparkling waters which please the young and gay. I am no longer young, and my heart, through weary years of mourning over the dead, is attuned to mirth. Moreover, the walls of my castle are broken. The shadows are many, and the wind breathes cold through the broken battlements and casements. I love the shade and the shadow, and would be alone with my thoughts when I may.' His cousin Nosferatu the Vampyr, who appeared both in Murnau's masterpiece *Nosferatu. Symphony of Terror* and again, more talkatively, in Werner Herzog's film, *Nosferatu,* has spoken movingly of his plight: 'Dying is cruelty against the unsuspecting but ... it is more cruel not to be able to die ... The absence of love is the most abject pain.'

It's even worse for lesbian vampires. There may be women (and men) who'd consider eternal damnation a price worth paying for the pleasure of spending several centuries as Catherine Deneuve's lover. (Faust sold his soul for a much shorter time and for arguably less). But it's really not worth it. Afterwards you find yourself, as Deneuve's blood-drinking companions did in *The Hunger,* stuck in a very tiny wooden box for countless, fully-conscious aeons of agonising undeadness. Just say no.

Immortality is tough even when you're an angel. There are two angels, Damiel and Cassiel, in Wim Wenders' sublime *Wings of Desire.* Damiel falls in love with a beautiful trapeze artist and runs away from eternity to join the human circus, gladly exchanging his wings for true love. But what of Cassiel, who is left behind? When the lovers finally meet, Cassiel is present. Trapped in his lonely monochrome world as his friend moves to passion and technicolour, Cassiel turns his face to the wall and screams in silent despair.

'Hope I die before I get old,' sang The Who, though they didn't really mean it. Maurice Chevalier reckoned: 'Old age isn't so bad when you consider the alternatives.' Yet it is often said that ageing is entirely worse than the alternative; that the opposite of life is not death but the torment of physical and mental decay.

We live in a culture obsessed with beauty and youth. Thanks to improvements in diet and medical technology, we are living longer than at any time in recorded history. But more and more of us are living in nursing homes. As geneticists race to find ways to extend human lifespan, they are — or should be — haunted by the story of the Struldbruggs.

These were the immortals encountered on the third voyage of *Gulliver's Travels*. When Gulliver first hears of the Struldbruggs, he is delighted and assumes that their lives must be rich with wisdom. Not quite. The Struldbruggs had been denied the gift of eternal youth to go with their longevity and had aged hideously: 'They were the most mortifying Sight I ever beheld, and the Women more horrible than the Men. Besides the usual Deformities in extreme old age, they acquired an additional Ghastliness in Proportion to their Number of Years, which is not to be described ... At Ninety they lose their Teeth and Hair; they have at that Age no Distinction of Taste, but eat and drink whatever they can get, without Relish or Appetite. The Diseases they were subject to still continue without increasing or diminishing. In talking they forget the common Appellation of Things, and the Names of Persons, even of those who are their nearest Friends and Relations. For the same Reason they never can amuse themselves with reading, because their Memory will not serve to carry them from the Beginning of a Sentence to the End; and by this Defect they are deprived of the only Entertainment whereof they might otherwise be capable.'

Rainer Maria Rilke wrote:

'I reproach all modern religions for having presented to their faithful the consolations and extenuations of death, instead of giving their souls the means of getting along with death and coming to an understanding of death, with its complete and unmasked cruelty.' He also observed: 'There is an element of death in life, and I am astonished that one pretends to ignore it: death, whose unpitying presence we experience in each turn of fortune we survive because we must learn how to die slowly. We must learn to die: all of life is in that.'

Not only is death inevitable; it seems, also, to be necessary. Fritjof Capra, in *The Turning Point*, describes what he called 'the proper perspective on the phenomenon of death'. Cyclical self-renewal is an essential aspect of living systems. Living structures are continually replaced with living organisms. 'Birth and death, therefore, now appear as a central aspect of self-organisation, the very essence of life. Indeed, all living things around us renew themselves all the time. 'If you stand in a meadow, at the edge of a hillside and look around carefully, almost everything you can catch sight of is in the process of dying.' But for every organism that dies another one is born. Death, then, is not the opposite of life but an essential aspect of it.

Sorry, Woody.

WEALTH

DECADENCE

Past Glory

STATE OF

Ghost Town

Y E S T E R D A Y

F O R E S T S   O F   C H A N G I N G

Cherish

Rampant
Rife
Run Riot

**GOOD
OLD DAYS**

Photos

Rituals

Mature
Wine
Full-bodied

Splendour

Abandoned

Stamping
Ground

Old Age

Retrospective

Moulds

C O L O U R

Strolling

Winkle

Shrink

Source

M O R T A

Paddle

Great Pleasure

Symbiosis

Flow

Peer

And Again

Discoloration

Relevant

Old Ideals

Irrelevant

Mistakes

Sigh

Quality

Transform

Memory

B A Y   O F   C O N T E N T M E N T

Happiness

D I G N I T Y

Snail's Pace

Again

All Day Long

Echo

Longing

Slow Stream

Awaken

PLEASURE

Sundays

Spree

R E M I N I S C E N C E

Requiem

R A M B L I N G

Lazing

Echo

Humming

Same Old Story
Frolic

C R U M B L I N G   C O A

Fa

Drift

Jump

Nostalgia

Steadfast

Experience

Relic

Sip

Memoir

Cheers!

Souvenir

Mirror

Superb

Drink Deeply

With Pleasure

Backward Glances

Flashback

Ogle

Python

Mmmm!

SCALE

10   20   30   40   50

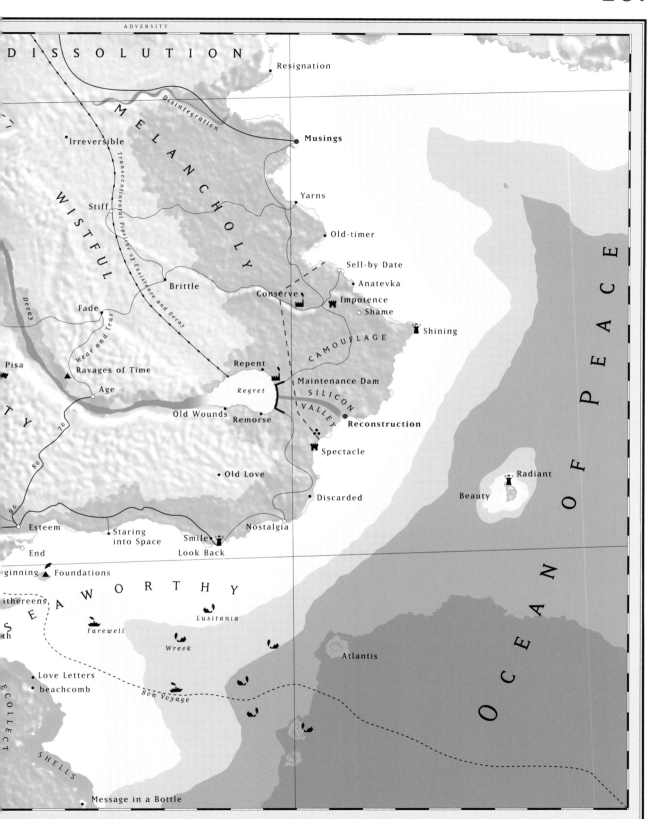

ADVERSITY

DISSOLUTION

MELANCHOLY

WISTFUL

• Resignation

Disintegration

• Irreversible

Transcontinental Pipeline of Existence and Decay

• Stiff

Musings

• Yarns

• Old-timer

• Sell-by Date

• Brittle

• Anatevka

Conserve

• Impotence

○ Shame

• Fade

Wear and Tear

CAMOUFLAGE

♗ Shining

Pisa

▲ Ravages of Time

○ Age

Regret

Repent

Maintenance Dam

SILICON

VALLEY

• Reconstruction

Decay

• Old Wounds

• Remorse

♜ Spectacle

• Old Love

Radiant

• Discarded

Beauty

○

70

• Esteem

• Staring
into Space

Smile

Nostalgia

○ End

Look Back

SEAWORTHY

80

90

ginning ▲ Foundations

ithereens

Lusitania

th

♖ Farewell

Wreck

• Love Letters

Atlantis

• beachcomb

Bon Voyage

ECOLLECT

SHELLS

• Message in a Bottle

OCEAN OF PEACE

'Death is the sound of distant thunder at a picnic.'
W. H. Auden

'Death is no more than passing from one room into another.'
Helen Keller

'It's tough to make predictions, especially about the future.'
Yogi Berra

Benjamin Franklin said death and taxes were the only certainties in life, but we will not experience our own death. 'Death is not an event in life,' wrote Wittgenstein. 'When we are there, death is not and when death is there we are not,' said Epicurus. So where does that leave us? Nowhere, as Epicurus would probably say a little too quickly. Wittgenstein would probably mumble something about not having the faintest idea and hold his tongue.

Death is the Great Unknown, and that does nothing to make it more popular. Unknown is unloved, after all. This would not be a problem if we could always keep it at a great distance. But we cannot. The presence of non-existence in existence, as Heidegger put it, haunts us constantly, like a shadow. We permanently risk vanishing into nothingness. And not only through death: isolation or total estrangement have a similar effect. The existential angst all this inspires need not be purely negative. It should persuade us not to squander our time, but to embrace life and to enjoy it to the full.

Near-death experiences have become a good deal more popular than death itself. People who have come back from near-misses with eternity have led us to believe our own deaths may not be so bad after all. Martha Todd, a professor of English literature at an American University, went into cardiac arrest due to an allergic reaction during a routine operation:

> I realised I was floating towards the ceiling. I could see everyone very clearly around the bed, even my own body. I thought it was strange that they were worrying about my body. I felt fine and I wanted them to know this, but there was no way in which I could make this clear to them. It was just as if a veil or a screen had been placed between me and the other people in the room. I became aware of an opening, if you can call it that. It seemed to be a deep, dark hole and I shot inside. I had no idea what was happening to me, but it was thrilling. I came through the tunnel to a place bathed in soft, bright light and filled with radiant love. This love was all around me and it even seemed to fill my deepest innerself. At a certain point, I was shown the events of my life. I was in a huge kind of

panorama. It is not really easy to explain. There were people with me in the light, people who had already died; a university friend, my grandfather, a great aunt and many others. They were radiant, happy. I did not want to go back, but a man in the light said I had to return, that I had not yet done what I had to do in life. I returned to my own body with a shock.

Other people who have spent more time in Elsewhere than Martha Todd have described how it looks. Although it is difficult for them to find the right words, these witnesses generally describe it as a delightful rural area, sometimes with beautifully coloured birds and flowers, intriguing scents, heavenly music. And there are people there: some who have already passed over, others, including friends, who are still alive, especially children.

With this alluring prospect, who wouldn't be tempted to exchange the temporary for the eternal? Yet very few of us are keen to experience it for ourselves. Is this because we do not really believe in Elsewhere and are therefore a little dubious about Near-elsewhere?

We all have our own reasons for being and for remaining here on earth. Our purpose is to pursue all that is good, true and beautiful; discover who we are; create a paradise on earth; fulfil our duty; serve God; serve our fellow humans; work out karma; earn our place in heaven; discover the divinity within ourselves. Alternatively, we must passively accept our fate and have a better time in the next life. Or — no less valuably — be part of something bigger than ourselves in politics, a career, as a lover, through having children.

In *God: A Biography*, the former Jesuit Jack Miles reached the conclusion that the Tanach, the Old Testament in its original Jewish version, showed that God had created humans in order to get to know Himself better, through His own experiences. Since all our experiences are unique, the purpose of our lives would thus be to have as many different experiences as possible in order that God would end up with a kind of Atlas of Experience.

For the moment, it's a good idea for us to get to know ourselves better, because our existence could turn into non-existence at any moment. Perhaps we can do this by examining whether our fear of Elsewhere and the Void is the Secret with which we drive away Boredom and dive into Passion, Knowledge, Mountains of Work or Pure Pleasure. Finally, we shall come Home, Recovered.

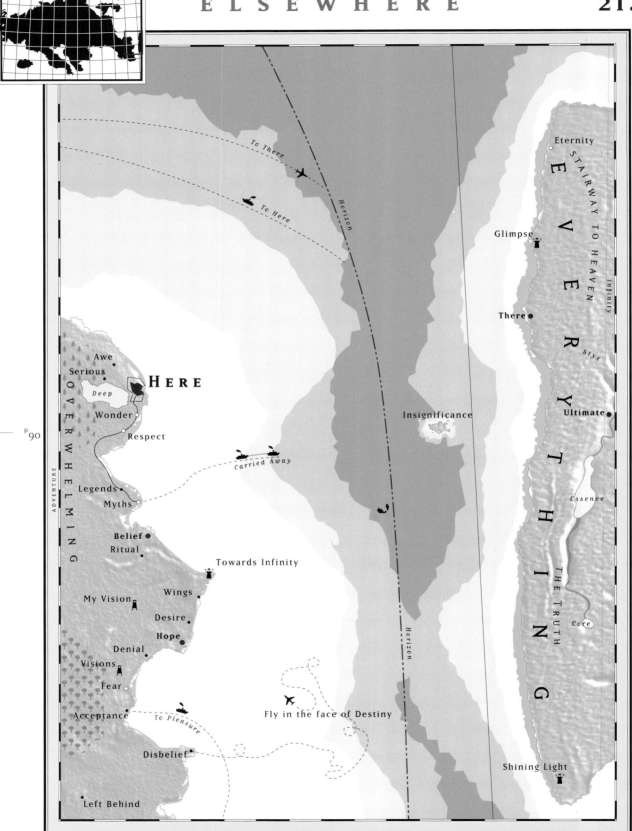

INDEX

p93